THE THEOLOGY OF LOVE IN THE TEN COMMANDMENTS

Dr. Maxwell Shimba

Printed in the United States of America

TABLE OF CONTENTS

INTRODUCTION

Theology of Love in the Ten Commandments

By Dr. Maxwell Shimba

The Ten Commandments stand as one of the most profound and enduring pillars of Judeo-Christian ethics. Given to Moses on Mount Sinai, these divine instructions have shaped the moral and spiritual foundations of countless generations. Often perceived as a set of rigid laws or strict rules to be followed, the Ten Commandments are, in essence, a divine expression of love—a roadmap for living a life rooted in love for God and for our fellow human beings.

In our modern world, where moral relativism and ethical ambiguity often reign, the Ten Commandments offer a timeless and clear moral compass. However, beyond their role as ethical guidelines, they embody a deeper, transformative truth: they are fundamentally about love. This book aims to explore the Ten Commandments through the lens of love, revealing how each commandment reflects and promotes a theology of love that is central to the Christian faith.

From the first commandment, which calls for exclusive devotion to God, to the tenth, which urges contentment and guards against covetousness, each directive encapsulates a specific aspect of love. The first four commandments focus on our relationship with God, emphasizing reverence, worship, and rest as expressions of our love and devotion to Him. The remaining six commandments address our relationships with others, highlighting respect, honor, fidelity, and integrity as manifestations of our love for our neighbors.

In examining the Ten Commandments, we will see that they are not merely prohibitions but positive calls to love more deeply and authentically. They guide us toward a life that mirrors God's love, fostering communities where love, respect, and justice prevail. This exploration will delve into the rich theological and practical implications of each commandment, offering insights into how we can embody this divine love in our daily lives.

Moreover, understanding the Ten Commandments as a unified theology of love provides a holistic perspective that can transform our approach to faith and ethics. It challenges us to move beyond mere compliance to a heartfelt embrace of the principles that underpin these commandments. In doing so, we draw closer to the essence of God's character and His vision for human flourishing.

The journey through the Ten Commandments as a theology of love invites us to reflect on our own lives and relationships. It encourages us to seek a deeper connection with God and a more profound love for others. As we embark on this exploration, may we discover anew the beauty and depth of God's love as revealed through His commandments, and may our hearts be inspired to live out this love in every aspect of our lives.

Dr. Maxwell Shimba

DR. MAXWELL SHIMBA

CHAPTER 01

INTRODUCTION

The Ten Commandments, given to Moses on Mount Sinai, are fundamental to Judeo-Christian ethics and theology. They are often viewed primarily as laws or rules to be followed. However, a deeper exploration reveals that they are profoundly rooted in the concept of love. This book aims to explore how each commandment embodies and promotes love, both for God and for fellow human beings.

The Significance of the Ten Commandments

The Ten Commandments, also known as the Decalogue, hold a central place in the religious traditions of Judaism and Christianity. Inscribed on two stone tablets, they were delivered to the Israelites at a critical moment in their history. These commandments were not just a set of laws but a covenantal framework establishing the relationship between God and His people. They were intended to guide the

Israelites in their worship and daily living, promoting a harmonious and just society.

The Commandments as Expressions of Love

While the Ten Commandments are often seen as legalistic decrees, their essence is rooted in love. Jesus Himself summarized the law and the prophets with the commands to love God and to love one's neighbor as oneself (Matthew 22:37-40). This summary encapsulates the heart of the Ten Commandments. The first four commandments focus on our relationship with God, emphasizing love and reverence for Him. The remaining six commandments address our interactions with others, promoting love, respect, and justice in human relationships.

Love for God: The First Four Commandments

The first commandment, "You shall have no other gods before me," establishes the foundation of exclusive devotion to God. This is the starting point of love— acknowledging God as the supreme being deserving of our utmost allegiance and affection. It calls us to prioritize our relationship with God above all else, reflecting a deep, personal love for Him.

The second commandment, "You shall not make for yourself a carved image," warns against idolatry. Idolatry distorts the true nature of God and diminishes our love for

Him. By worshiping God as He is, without reducing Him to an image or idol, we preserve the purity of our relationship with Him, expressing our love through true worship.

The third commandment, "You shall not take the name of the Lord your God in vain," speaks to the reverence and respect we should have for God's name. Using God's name with respect and honor reflects our love and reverence for Him. It acknowledges His holiness and our deep regard for His identity.

The fourth commandment, "Remember the Sabbath day, to keep it holy," is a command to rest in God. The Sabbath is a gift of rest, reflecting God's love and care for us. By observing the Sabbath, we express our love for God, trust in His provision, and acknowledge the value of rest and worship in our lives. It is a day set apart to reconnect with God and to reflect on His goodness.

Love for Others: The Remaining Six Commandments

The fifth commandment, "Honor your father and your mother," underscores the importance of family and the respect and love owed to parents. It establishes a framework for loving relationships within the family unit, promoting harmony and respect. Honoring parents is an expression of love and gratitude for their role in our lives.

The sixth commandment, "You shall not murder," reflects the sanctity of human life. This commandment embodies God's love for every individual and calls us to value and protect life. It fosters a community where love and respect for life prevail, upholding the dignity and worth of every person.

The seventh commandment, "You shall not commit adultery," speaks to marital fidelity as a profound expression of love and commitment. This commandment protects the sanctity of marriage, encouraging trust, loyalty, and love between spouses. It underscores the importance of faithfulness in loving relationships.

The eighth commandment, "You shall not steal," promotes respect for others' property. Respecting others' property is an act of love and consideration. It acknowledges the rights and dignity of others, fostering a community based on trust and mutual respect.

The ninth commandment, "You shall not bear false witness against your neighbor," emphasizes truthfulness as a cornerstone of loving relationships. This commandment promotes honesty and integrity, essential for trust and love within any community. It calls us to be truthful and fair in our dealings with others.

The tenth commandment, "You shall not covet," encourages contentment and guards against envy and greed. Contentment reflects a heart at peace, free from the destructive nature of covetousness. This commandment urges us to appreciate what we have and to cultivate a loving and grateful heart.

A Unified Theology of Love

The Ten Commandments, when viewed through the lens of love, reveal a divine blueprint for a life rooted in love for God and for others. They guide us in building a society where love, respect, and reverence are foundational principles. By embracing the love inherent in these commandments, we draw closer to understanding the heart of God and living out His greatest commandments: to love Him and to love our neighbors as ourselves.

In the chapters that follow, we will explore each commandment in detail, uncovering the profound ways in which they reflect and promote a theology of love. We will delve into the rich theological and practical implications of each commandment, offering insights into how we can embody this divine love in our daily lives. Through this journey, may we discover anew the beauty and depth of God's love as revealed through His commandments, and may our hearts be inspired to live out this love in every aspect of our lives.

CHAPTER 02

THE FIRST COMMANDMENTS: LOVE AND ALLEGIANCE TO GOD

"You shall have no other gods before me."

(Exodus 20:3)

The first commandment is foundational to the entire Decalogue. It calls for exclusive devotion to the one true God, Yahweh, and serves as the bedrock upon which all other commandments stand. This commandment is more than a prohibition against idolatry; it is an invitation to enter into a profound, loving relationship with God, marked by trust, loyalty, and unreserved allegiance.

The Historical Context

To fully appreciate the significance of the First Commandment, we must understand the historical and cultural context in which it was given. The Israelites had just been delivered from centuries of slavery in Egypt, a land dominated by a pantheon of gods and goddesses. In this polytheistic environment, the worship of multiple deities was the norm. The commandment, therefore, was a radical call to monotheism—a revolutionary declaration that Yahweh alone is God.

By asserting His exclusive sovereignty, God was establishing a new identity for the Israelites. They were to be a people set apart, dedicated wholly to Him. This exclusivity was not just about worship practices; it was about recognizing God's unique role as the Creator, Sustainer, and Redeemer. It was about forming a covenantal relationship characterized by love and faithfulness.

Exclusive Devotion as an Act of Love

At its core, the first commandment is a call to love. It demands that we place God at the center of our lives, acknowledging His supremacy and prioritizing our relationship with Him above all else. This exclusive devotion is the foundation of genuine love—a love that is undivided and wholehearted.

In human relationships, true love often requires exclusivity. Just as a married couple pledges fidelity to one another, forsaking all others, so too are we called to pledge our fidelity to God. This exclusive devotion reflects a deep love for Him, a love that recognizes His worthiness and responds with complete commitment.

Trust and Loyalty in Our Relationship with God

The first commandment also underscores the importance of trust and loyalty in our relationship with God. To have "no other gods" means to place our complete trust in Him alone. It means relying on His provision, wisdom, and guidance, and not turning to other sources for what only He can provide.

In a world filled with competing loyalties and distractions, maintaining this exclusive devotion requires intentionality. It calls us to examine our hearts and identify anything that might rival our allegiance to God. Whether it be wealth, power, relationships, or personal ambitions, anything that takes precedence over God becomes an idol in our lives.

Loyalty to God involves a steadfast commitment to His ways and His purposes. It means aligning our values, decisions, and actions with His will, even when it is challenging. This loyalty is a testament to our love for God, demonstrating that we trust Him above all else and are committed to following Him faithfully.

The Challenge of Modern Idolatry

While the first commandment was given in a context of overt idol worship, its relevance remains undiminished today. Modern idolatry may not involve carved images or pagan gods, but it manifests in subtler, yet equally insidious, forms. Materialism, consumerism, careerism, and the pursuit of personal success can all become idols that vie for our devotion.

In today's fast-paced, achievement-oriented society, the temptation to prioritize worldly pursuits over our relationship with God is ever-present. The first commandment challenges us to resist these temptations and to continually reaffirm our allegiance to God. It calls us to evaluate our priorities and ensure that nothing supersedes our love and devotion to Him.

Living Out the First Commandment

Living out the first commandment involves cultivating a deep, personal relationship with God. It means spending time in prayer, worship, and the study of His Word. It involves seeking His guidance in all aspects of our lives and striving to align our will with His.

Practically, this might mean setting aside regular times for prayer and reflection, participating in communal worship, and being part of a faith community that encourages spiritual growth. It involves making choices that honor God and reflect our commitment to Him, whether in our personal lives, our relationships, or our professional endeavors.

Moreover, living out this commandment involves a continual process of self-examination and repentance. It means being vigilant against anything that might encroach upon our exclusive devotion to God and being willing to turn away from those things that hinder our relationship with Him.

The Fruit of Exclusive Devotion

When we embrace the first commandment and live out our exclusive devotion to God, we experience the profound fruit of this relationship. We find a deep sense of peace and fulfillment that comes from knowing and loving the one true God. We experience His faithfulness and provision in our lives, and we grow in our ability to trust Him in all circumstances.

This exclusive devotion also transforms our relationships with others. As we grow in our love for God, we become more capable of loving others selflessly and sacrificially. Our relationships are enriched as we reflect God's love and faithfulness in our interactions with those around us.

The first commandment, "You shall have no other gods before me," is a powerful call to love and allegiance to God. It establishes the foundation for a relationship built on trust, loyalty, and exclusive devotion. By prioritizing our relationship with God above all else, we align our lives with His purposes and experience the fullness of His love.

As we journey through the Ten Commandments, let us remember that at the heart of these divine instructions is a call to love—love for God and love for our neighbors. May we respond to this call with hearts fully devoted to Him, living out His commandments in ways that reflect His love and bring glory to His name.

EXPOSITORY STUDY AND COMPREHENSIVE COMMENTARY VERSE 3

Verse 3:

"Thou shalt have no other gods before me."

King James Bible's Reference:

"Thou shalt have no other gods before me." (Exodus 20:3, KJV)

Interpretation:

This verse is the first of the Ten Commandments, directly addressing the exclusivity of worship due to Yahweh, the God of Israel. It establishes the fundamental principle of monotheism in Israel's religious practice, emphasizing that God demands undivided allegiance and prohibits the worship of other gods.

Commentary:

Contextual Overview:

Exodus 20 marks the covenant at Mount Sinai where God establishes His laws with the people of Israel. This first commandment sets the tone for the relationship between God and His people, highlighting His sovereignty and the expectation of loyalty from His followers.

"Thou shalt have no other gods before me":

- Exclusive Worship: This commandment underscores the exclusive worship that is due to God alone. The phrase "before me" can also be interpreted as "beside me" or "in my presence," which rules out the worship of any other deity alongside Yahweh.

- Foundation of Monotheism: This command establishes the foundational aspect of monotheism in the Israelite religion. It not only commands the worship of one God but also the rejection of all others.

- Relationship and Loyalty: This commandment speaks to the relational aspect between God and His people. It emphasizes that their allegiance to Him must be undivided, reflecting covenantal loyalty.

Concordance:

- Deuteronomy 5:7: "Thou shalt have none other gods before me." (Reiteration in Deuteronomy, emphasizing the continuity of this command across different texts and contexts.)

- Deuteronomy 6:14-15: "Ye shall not go after other gods, of the gods of the people which are round about you; (For the LORD thy God is a jealous God among you) lest the anger of the LORD thy God be kindled against thee, and destroy thee from off the face of the earth."

- Matthew 4:10: "Then saith Jesus unto him, Get thee hence, Satan: for it is written, Thou shalt worship the Lord thy God, and him only shalt thou serve." (This New Testament reference reiterates the exclusive worship of God, endorsed by Jesus.)

Interpretation and Application:

- Foundation of Faith: This commandment is foundational to the Judeo-Christian understanding of God. It forms the basis for the exclusivity of faith in one God and informs the worship practices of believers.

- Against Idolatry: It explicitly forbids idolatry, which was a common practice among the nations surrounding Israel. This command helps distinguish the Israelites from other cultures by their worship practices.

- Modern Implications: In contemporary terms, this commandment challenges believers to examine what they prioritize in their lives, urging them to place God above all else, which could include modern "idols" such as materialism, power, or even relationships.

This verse and its commandment are pivotal in understanding the entire biblical narrative of God's relationship with humanity, highlighting themes of loyalty, faith, and the sanctity of divine worship.

Exploring the theme of exclusive worship and the prohibition against idolatry throughout Scripture offers a rich understanding of how these concepts develop and their implications for both historical and contemporary faith practices.

1. Development in the Old Testament:

- Deuteronomy 6:4-5 ("Hear, O Israel: The Lord our God, the Lord is one. Love the Lord your God with all your heart and with all your soul and with all your strength."):

This is known as the Shema, central to Jewish prayer services, emphasizing monotheism and total devotion to Yahweh alone, which is a direct extension of the first commandment.

- Isaiah 44:9-20:

This passage mocks the folly of idol making, illustrating the irrationality of crafting idols from the same material used for everyday purposes like cooking and then worshiping them. It underscores the uniqueness of God as the only living God, in stark contrast to lifeless idols.

2. Reaffirmation in the New Testament:

- Matthew 22:37-38 ("Jesus replied: 'Love the Lord your God with all your heart and with all your soul and with all your mind. This is the first and greatest commandment.'"):

Jesus reaffirms the Old Testament command to love God exclusively and wholeheartedly, emphasizing that this is the greatest commandment.

- 1 Corinthians 10:14-22:

Paul warns against idolatry by comparing the Lord's Supper to pagan sacrifice rituals, highlighting that Christians cannot partake of both the table of the Lord and the table of demons, emphasizing exclusivity in Christian worship.

3. Practical Applications Today:

- Identifying Modern Idols:

In contemporary settings, idols can be anything that takes priority over God in our lives. This could be money, relationships, career, or even technology and social media. Recognizing these helps in realigning our priorities to ensure God remains supreme.

- Living Out the Commandment:

Practically, living out this commandment means regular self-examination of our actions and desires to ensure they align with God's will. Engaging in regular worship, prayer, and reading of Scripture helps maintain focus on God.

- Community and Worship:

Just as the early Christians gathered in Solomon's Porch for communal worship, modern believers are called to community worship that strengthens faith and accountability to God's commands. This also serves as a witness to the world of the power of God's truth.

4. Theological Reflection:

- God's Jealousy and Love:

God's command for exclusive worship is rooted in His character as a jealous God (Exodus 34:14). This jealousy is not petty but stems from His deep love for His people and His desire for their undivided love and commitment.

- Holiness and Separation:

This command also sets believers apart from the world, calling for a distinctive lifestyle that honors God. It's about holiness and being set apart for divine purposes, which reflects God's own holiness.

By tracing the development of this theme through Scripture and considering its practical implications, believers are invited to deepen their understanding of God's nature and their relationship with Him. Each aspect of Scripture that touches on this command provides insights into living a life that truly honors God as the only one deserving of worship.

CHAPTER 03

THE SECOND COMMANDMENT: LOVE THROUGH WORSHIP

"You shall not make for yourself a carved image, or any likeness of anything that is in heaven above, or that is in the earth beneath, or that is in the water under the earth. You shall not bow down to them or serve them, for I the Lord your God am a jealous God, visiting the iniquity of the fathers on the children to the third and the fourth generation of those who hate me, but showing steadfast love to thousands of those who love me and keep my commandments."

(Exodus 20:4-6)

The second commandment is a clear prohibition against idolatry, which was a prevalent practice in the ancient world. Idolatry involves the creation and worship of physical representations of gods, which stand in stark contrast to the worship of the one true God. This commandment is not merely a ban on a particular religious practice; it is a profound declaration of how we should love and worship God. It emphasizes the importance of worshiping God as He is, without reducing Him to a finite image or idol, thus preserving the purity and integrity of our relationship with Him.

Understanding Idolatry

Idolatry, in its most basic sense, is the act of giving honor, worship, or reverence to anything other than God. In the context of the Israelites, this often involved the creation of physical idols—statues or images that were believed to embody or represent deities. These idols were seen as tangible objects of worship, but they inevitably diminished the infinite and transcendent nature of God.

The danger of idolatry lies in its distortion of God's true nature. An idol, no matter how grand or beautifully crafted, can never capture the fullness of who God is. It limits our understanding and relationship with Him, reducing the infinite to the finite. Idolatry misrepresents God and leads people away from a genuine relationship with Him.

The Jealousy of God

In the second commandment, God describes Himself as a "jealous God." This divine jealousy is not akin to human envy or insecurity; rather, it reflects God's deep desire for an exclusive relationship with His people. God's jealousy is rooted in His love for us and His knowledge that idolatry leads us away from the true source of life and love.

God's jealousy is a protective love. Just as a loving spouse desires fidelity and exclusivity in marriage, God desires our undivided worship and loyalty. This commandment highlights the relational nature of our connection with God. It is not about legalistic adherence to rules, but about maintaining a pure and devoted relationship with our Creator.

Worshiping God in Spirit and Truth

Jesus reiterated the essence of the second commandment when He spoke to the Samaritan woman at the well. He said, "God is spirit, and those who worship him must worship in spirit and truth" (John 4:24). This statement underscores the need for authentic worship that transcends physical forms and focuses on the true nature of God.

Worshiping God in spirit and truth means engaging with Him on a deeper, more intimate level. It involves recognizing His omnipresence, omniscience, and omnipotence, and approaching Him with a heart full of love, reverence, and humility. True worship is not confined to rituals or physical symbols; it is a heartfelt response to God's love and greatness.

The Pitfalls of Modern Idolatry

While few people today worship carved images, idolatry is still a pervasive issue. Modern idols may not be statues of gods, but they take many other forms. Money, power, status, relationships, technology, and even self can become objects of worship when they occupy the central place in our lives that belongs to God alone.

Modern idolatry often manifests in the pursuit of material success, the desire for social recognition, or the dependence on technology and entertainment for fulfillment. These idols promise satisfaction and meaning, but they ultimately leave us empty, as they cannot fulfill the deep spiritual needs that only God can satisfy.

The second commandment challenges us to examine our hearts and identify anything that competes with our devotion to God. It calls us to reject these idols and turn our hearts fully toward Him. This involves a conscious decision to prioritize our relationship with God above all else and to seek Him as the ultimate source of our identity and purpose.

Preserving the Purity of Our Relationship with God

Worshiping God without idols preserves the purity of our relationship with Him. It ensures that our understanding of God is not tainted by human limitations or misconceptions. When we worship God as He is, we open ourselves to experiencing His true nature and the fullness of His love.

This commandment also teaches us about the nature of true love. True love does not seek to control or manipulate; it honors and respects the other as they are. By worshiping God without idols, we honor Him as He is, without trying to confine Him to our limited understanding.

Moreover, this pure worship fosters a deeper intimacy with God. When we approach God without the intermediary of idols, we encounter Him more directly and personally. This deepens our relationship with Him and allows us to experience His presence and guidance in our lives more profoundly.

The Generational Impact of Worship

The second commandment includes a warning about the consequences of idolatry and a promise of blessing for those who love God and keep His commandments. God speaks of visiting "the iniquity of the fathers on the children to the third and the fourth generation of those who hate me, but showing steadfast love to thousands of those who love me and keep my commandments" (Exodus 20:5-6).

This highlights the generational impact of our worship. Idolatry can lead to spiritual and moral decay that affects not only individuals but also families and communities.

Conversely, a legacy of true worship and love for God brings blessings that extend far beyond our lifetimes. When we worship God faithfully, we set an example for future generations, fostering a heritage of faith and devotion.

Living Out the Second Commandment

To live out the second commandment, we must cultivate a practice of worship that is centered on the true nature of God. This involves regular engagement with Scripture, prayer, and reflection, allowing us to grow in our understanding of who God is. It also means participating in communal worship and fellowship, where we can encourage one another to remain faithful and avoid the pitfalls of idolatry.

Practically, this might involve simplifying our lives to remove distractions and idols, dedicating time each day to focus on God, and being mindful of how we invest our resources and attention. It calls for a heart that continually seeks God and values His presence above all else.

The second commandment, "You shall not make for yourself a carved image," is a powerful directive that calls us to worship God in spirit and truth. It warns against the distortions of idolatry and invites us into a pure, intimate relationship with God. By rejecting idols and focusing our worship on God alone, we preserve the integrity of our relationship with Him and experience the fullness of His love.

As we continue to explore the Ten Commandments, let us remember that each commandment is rooted in the theology of love. The second commandment, in particular, teaches us about the nature of true worship and the importance of loving God as He is. May we respond to this call with hearts devoted to worshiping God in spirit and truth, allowing His love to transform our lives and our communities.

EXPOSITORY STUDY AND COMPREHENSIVE COMMENTARY VERSE 4-6

Expository study and comprehensive commentary on Exodus 20:4-6 using the King James Bible. These verses form part of the Ten Commandments, specifically focusing on the prohibition against idolatry.

Verses 4-6:

"Thou shalt not make unto thee any graven image or any likeness of anything that is in heaven above, or that is in the earth beneath, or that is in the water under the earth: Thou shalt not bow down thyself to them, nor serve them: for I the LORD thy God am a jealous God, visiting the iniquity of the fathers upon the children unto the third and fourth generation of them that hate me; And shewing mercy unto thousands of them that love me, and keep my commandments."

King James Bible's References:

- Exodus 20:4-6 (as cited)

Interpretation:

Verse 4: "Thou shalt not make unto thee any graven image, or any likeness of anything that is in heaven above, or that is in the earth beneath, or that is in the water under the earth:"

- This commandment prohibits the making of idols or images intended for worship. It reflects God's desire for His people to worship Him in spirit and truth, without the aid or representation of physical images which was common in neighboring pagan cultures.

Verse 5: "Thou shalt not bow down thyself to them, nor serve them: for I the LORD thy God am a jealous God, visiting the iniquity of the fathers upon the children unto the third and fourth generation of them that hate me;"

- Worship and service are to be directed to God alone. The reference to God as a "jealous God" emphasizes His demand for exclusive devotion. The consequences of idolatry are severe, impacting not only the individual but also extending to future generations, illustrating the serious social and spiritual repercussions of idolatry.

Verse 6: "And shewing mercy unto thousands of them that love me, and keep my commandments."

- In contrast to the punishment for idolatry, this verse highlights God's mercy toward those who love Him and obey His commandments. The promise extends far beyond the immediate family, suggesting a legacy of blessing for those faithful to God.

Commentary and Concordance:

- Exodus 34:7: "Keeping mercy for thousands, forgiving iniquity and transgression and sin, and that will by no means clear the guilty; visiting the iniquity of the fathers upon the children, and upon the children's children, unto the third and to the fourth generation."

- Deuteronomy 5:8-10: "Thou shalt not make thee any graven image, or any likeness of any thing that is in heaven above, or that is in the earth beneath, or that is in the waters beneath the earth: Thou shalt not bow down thyself unto them, nor serve them: for I the LORD thy God am a jealous God, visiting the iniquity of the fathers upon the children unto the third and fourth generation of them that hate me, And shewing mercy unto thousands of them that love me and keep my commandments."

- Deuteronomy 27:15: "Cursed be the man that maketh any graven or molten image, an abomination unto the

LORD, the work of the hands of the craftsman, and putteth it in a secret place. And all the people shall answer and say, Amen."

Interpretation and Application:

- Exclusive Worship: The commandments emphasize that worship should be directed exclusively to God without the intermediation of images, reflecting a fundamental principle of monotheistic faith.

- Intergenerational Impact: The effects of idolatry underscore the intergenerational impact of sin, indicating the importance of spiritual fidelity for the well-being of future generations.

- Mercy and Obedience: The promise of mercy to those who obey God highlights the blessings associated with fidelity to God's commandments, serving as an encouragement for adherence to God's laws.

Let's delve deeper into each aspect of Exodus 20:4-6 to better understand the theological and practical implications of this commandment against idolatry.

1. The Prohibition of Idols (Verse 4)

- Theological Implications: The prohibition against making graven images reflects the invisible and incomprehensible nature of God. Unlike the pagan deities of surrounding cultures, which were often represented in physical forms, the God of Israel transcends physical representation. This commandment emphasizes the distinctiveness of Yahweh and sets the foundation for a relationship based on faith and trust rather than on sensory experience.

- Practical Applications: For the Israelites, this commandment meant avoiding the worship practices of their neighbors, which could lead to syncretism—a blending of religious practices that would dilute their faith. For modern believers, this extends to avoiding the modern "idols" of materialism, status, or anything else that might take precedence over their relationship with God.

2. Jealousy of God and Consequences of Idolatry (Verse 5)

- Theological Implications: The jealousy of God is not like human jealousy, which is often self-serving. Instead, it's a zeal for the well-being of His people, ensuring they do not divert their allegiance to what would harm them. The consequences laid out for idolatry (affecting up to the third and fourth generations) illustrate the severe social and spiritual decay that idolatry can introduce into a community.

- Practical Applications: This highlights the importance of spiritual vigilance and the responsibilities of each generation to the next. Parents and community leaders are reminded of their role in setting a spiritual example and not leading future generations into practices that lead away from God.

3. Promise of Mercy (Verse 6)

- Theological Implications: The contrast between the punitive measures against those who hate God and the mercy shown to thousands who love Him and keep His commandments reinforces the character of God as just but also extremely gracious. The "thousands" signifies a much greater number, emphasizing God's preference for mercy over judgment.

- Practical Applications: This serves as an encouragement for fidelity and obedience. It reassures believers that their efforts to live according to God's commandments are recognized and will be rewarded, not just in their own lives but extending to many generations. This long-term view of God's blessings encourages a commitment that transcends immediate circumstances.

Broader Context and Modern Relevance

- Community and Law: These commandments were not just about religious observance but about maintaining the social and spiritual fabric of the community. They helped forge a distinct identity for Israel among the nations.

- Modern Idolatry: In a contemporary context, idolatry can be understood as giving ultimate importance to anything other than God. This can be career, relationships, achievements, or even technology and social media. The principles derived from these verses encourage believers to evaluate what occupies the "throne" of their lives.

Reflective Questions

- Are there areas in my life where something other than God receives my primary energy, resources, or affection?

- How do I cultivate a community or family life that honors these principles and sets a foundation for future generations?

Exploring these verses deeply offers rich insights into God's character and His desires for His people, along with practical ways to apply these truths in everyday life. If you have specific aspects you'd like to explore further or any additional questions, feel free to ask!

CHAPTER 04

THE THIRD COMMANDMENT: LOVE AND REVERENCE FOR GOD'S NAME

"You shall not take the name of the Lord your God in vain, for the Lord will not hold him guiltless who takes his name in vain."

(Exodus 20:7)

The third commandment addresses the importance of respecting God's name. In a world where words are often taken lightly, this commandment stands as a powerful reminder of the weight and significance of how we speak about God. Respecting God's name is more than a prohibition against careless speech; it is a profound act of love and reverence. This commandment signifies our acknowledgment of God's holiness, authority, and the deep respect we owe Him.

The Meaning of God's Name

In ancient times, a name was not merely a label but a representation of one's character, reputation, and essence. This is especially true of God's name, which encompasses His nature, power, and presence. In the Bible, God's name reveals His attributes and His relationship with His people. For example, names like Yahweh (I AM), Elohim (God), and Adonai (Lord) each convey different aspects of God's identity and His covenantal relationship with humanity.

Taking God's name in vain involves using it in a manner that is empty, frivolous, or disrespectful. This can include cursing, false swearing, or any casual or irreverent use of God's name. Such misuse diminishes the reverence due to God and undermines the sacredness of His name.

Reverence as an Expression of Love

Respecting God's name is a natural expression of love and reverence. When we truly love someone, we speak of them with honor and respect. Our words reflect our relationship and the value we place on that person. Similarly, how we use God's name reflects our love and respect for Him.

Reverence for God's name acknowledges His holiness and our deep regard for His authority. It recognizes that God is not just another figure in our lives but the sovereign Creator and Sustainer of all things. This reverence shapes our attitudes and actions, reminding us of our place before Him and the honor due to His name.

The Holiness of God's Name

The concept of holiness is central to understanding the third commandment. Holiness means being set apart, unique, and pure. God's name is holy because He is holy. In the Lord's Prayer, Jesus taught us to pray, "Hallowed be your name" (Matthew 6:9), emphasizing the importance of recognizing and honoring the sanctity of God's name.

When we take God's name in vain, we profane what is holy, treating it as common or insignificant. This is not just a matter of etiquette but a violation of the sacred relationship we have with God. It reflects a lack of understanding and appreciation of His holiness.

The Power of Words

Words have immense power. They can build up or tear down, bless or curse, honor or disrespect. The Bible repeatedly emphasizes the importance of our speech and the impact it has on our lives and relationships. In Proverbs 18:21, we read, "Death and life are in the power of the tongue, and those who love it will eat its fruits."

Taking God's name in vain reflects a misuse of the power of words. It diminishes the sacred and undermines the respect and reverence that God deserves. Conversely, using

God's name with reverence and honor can deepen our relationship with Him and with others.

Living Out the Third Commandment

Living out the third commandment involves more than avoiding explicit misuse of God's name. It calls us to cultivate a heart and mind that continually honor God in our speech and actions. This can be practiced in several ways:

1. Mindful Speech: Being conscious of how we use God's name in everyday conversation. Avoiding casual or irreverent mentions and instead using His name with purpose and respect.

2. Truthful Oaths: If we invoke God's name to affirm truth or make promises, we must ensure that our words are truthful and our commitments are honored. False swearing or breaking vows made in God's name is a serious offense.

3. Praise and Worship: Using God's name in worship and praise with sincerity and reverence. Whether in prayer, song, or proclamation, our expressions of worship should reflect our deep love and respect for God.

4. Teaching and Witnessing: Speaking of God accurately and reverently when sharing our faith with others. Our testimony should honor God's name and reflect His true character.

The Consequences of Disrespect

The commandment comes with a solemn warning: "The Lord will not hold him guiltless who takes his name in vain." This underscores the seriousness with which God views the misuse of His name. Disrespecting God's name has consequences, both spiritual and communal. It can erode our relationship with God and diminish our witness to others.

However, this commandment also invites us to experience the blessings of honoring God's name. When we speak and act with reverence for God, we align ourselves with His holiness and experience a deeper connection with Him. Our lives become a testimony to His greatness, drawing others to the truth of His love and power.

The Broader Implications

Respecting God's name also has broader implications for how we view and treat others. Every person is created in the image of God and bears His likeness. Therefore, how we speak about and to others can reflect our reverence for God. Using words that build up, encourage, and honor others is a way of honoring God.

Moreover, our reverence for God's name extends to how we live our lives. Our actions should align with the values and principles that God's name represents. Living with integrity, justice, compassion, and love reflects the character of the God whose name we bear.

The third commandment, "You shall not take the name of the Lord your God in vain," calls us to a deep reverence and respect for God's name. This commandment is an act of love, reflecting our acknowledgment of His holiness and authority. By honoring God's name in our speech and actions, we cultivate a relationship with Him that is rooted in love and reverence.

As we continue to explore the Ten Commandments, we see that each commandment is a guide to living a life of love—love for God and love for others. The third commandment teaches us about the power of words and the importance of speaking and living in a way that honors God. May we strive to live out this commandment with hearts full of love and reverence, bringing glory to God's holy name in all that we do.

EXPOSITORY STUDY AND COMPREHENSIVE COMMENTARY VERSE 7

Verse 7:

"Thou shalt not take the name of the LORD thy God in vain; for the LORD will not hold him guiltless that taketh his name in vain."

King James Bible's Reference:

"Thou shalt not take the name of the LORD thy God in vain; for the LORD will not hold him guiltless that taketh his name in vain." (Exodus 20:7, KJV)

Interpretation:

This verse is the third of the Ten Commandments, focusing on the proper respect and use of God's name. It prohibits using the Lord's name in a frivolous or disrespectful manner, underscoring the holiness of God and the seriousness with which His name should be treated.

Commentary:

"Thou shalt not take the name of the LORD thy God in vain": To "take in vain" means to use something without due consideration for its significance or worth, particularly in a way that is empty, idle, or insincere. This commandment prohibits such misuse of God's name, which includes casual or disrespectful swearing and false oaths. It reflects the reverence due to God and His name, which symbolizes His character and authority (Leviticus 19:12; Matthew 5:33-37).

"For the LORD will not hold him guiltless that taketh his name in vain": This part of the verse emphasizes that there are consequences for misusing God's name. It serves as a warning of divine judgment, indicating that God takes this offense seriously and will not consider it a minor matter (Deuteronomy 5:11).

Concordance:

- Thou shalt not take the name of the LORD thy God in vain: This phrase emphasizes the importance of treating God's name with the utmost respect and reverence, prohibiting any form of misuse (Leviticus 19:12; Matthew 5:33-37).

- For the LORD will not hold him guiltless that taketh his name in vain: This statement warns of the serious consequences and divine judgment for those who misuse God's name, reinforcing the gravity of the commandment (Deuteronomy 5:11).

References from the King James Bible:

1. Leviticus 19:12: "And ye shall not swear by my name falsely, neither shalt thou profane the name of thy God: I am the LORD."

2. Matthew 5:33-37: "Again, ye have heard that it hath been said by them of old time, Thou shalt not forswear thyself, but shalt perform unto the Lord thine oaths: But I say unto you, Swear not at all; neither by heaven; for it is God's throne: Nor by the earth; for it is his footstool: neither by Jerusalem; for it is the city of the great King. Neither shalt thou swear by thy head, because thou canst not make one hair white or black. But let your communication be, Yea, yea; Nay, nay: for whatsoever is more than these cometh of evil."

3. Deuteronomy 5:11: "Thou shalt not take the name of the LORD thy God in vain: for the LORD will not hold him guiltless that taketh his name in vain."

Interpretation and Application:

- Reverence for God's Name: This commandment highlights the need for reverence and respect for God's name, reflecting the holiness and authority of God. It teaches that God's name should not be used lightly or disrespectfully in any context.

- Integrity in Speech: The prohibition against taking God's name in vain also calls for integrity in speech and truthfulness in oaths. It encourages believers to speak truthfully and sincerely without resorting to frivolous or false swearing.

- Awareness of Divine Judgment: The warning of divine judgment for misusing God's name serves as a reminder of God's justice and the seriousness with which He regards purity in speech and reverence towards Him.

Certainly! Let's delve deeper into the implications and broader context of Exodus 20:7, focusing on why the proper use of God's name is so important and how this commandment extends to various aspects of life and faith.

1. The Sanctity of God's Name

The commandment in Exodus 20:7 stresses the sanctity and holiness of God's name. In biblical culture, a name wasn't just a label but was thought to encompass the very essence of a person's character and identity. When it comes to God, His name represents His presence, power, and promises. Therefore, using His name in vain not only shows disrespect but also diminishes the reverence due to Him. This principle helps cultivate an attitude of respect and awe towards God and His divine attributes.

2. Ethical Speech and Conduct

This commandment has a direct impact on ethical speech and conduct among believers. By prohibiting the misuse of God's name, it also implicitly calls for truthfulness and integrity. In Matthew 5:33-37, Jesus expands on this commandment by advising against making oaths at all, suggesting that one's word should be enough—yes should mean yes, and no should mean no. This teaches that honesty should permeate the believer's actions and words, reflecting the character of God in everyday interactions.

3. Legal and Social Justice

In a judicial context, swearing falsely by God's name could pervert the course of justice, leading to wrongful punishment or the escape of the guilty. The commandment, therefore, has social justice implications, ensuring that justice is based on truth. It supports the broader biblical themes of justice and righteousness, emphasizing that society should operate on the principles of truth and fairness.

4. Spiritual Discipline and Worship

The third commandment also affects worship practices and spiritual discipline. It calls for sincerity in worship, where using God's name isn't just a ritualistic practice but a meaningful expression of genuine faith. This idea is mirrored in how Jesus criticized the Pharisees for their outward piety but inner spiritual emptiness (Matthew 15:8). Thus, this command teaches that worship should be heartfelt and genuine, not empty or manipulative.

5. Cultural and Educational Influence

Throughout history, this commandment has influenced cultural norms and educational practices in societies shaped by Judeo-Christian values. It has fostered a culture of respect for the divine and sacred things, often extending to how religious texts are handled and how religious discussions are conducted.

6. Modern Applications

In contemporary terms, this commandment challenges today's believers to consider how they invoke God's name in media, literature, and everyday conversation. It raises questions about the casual use of divine references in jokes, curses, or trivial matters, urging a thoughtful and reverent attitude.

The commandment not to take the Lord's name in vain continues to be relevant, teaching us about the sanctity of God's name, the importance of integrity, the foundations of justice, the depth of worship, and the respectful use of language. It's a comprehensive directive that affects both personal faith and communal life, encouraging a profound respect for God and His holiness.

CHAPTER 05

THE FOURTH COMMANDMENT: LOVE AND REST IN GOD

"Remember the Sabbath day, to keep it holy. Six days you shall labor, and do all your work, but the seventh day is a Sabbath to the Lord your God. On it you shall not do any work, you, or your son, or your daughter, your male servant, or your female servant, or your livestock, or the sojourner who is within your gates. For in six days the Lord made heaven and earth, the sea, and all that is in them, and rested on the seventh day. Therefore the Lord blessed the Sabbath day and made it holy."

(Exodus 20:8-11)

The fourth commandment introduces the Sabbath, a day set apart for rest and worship. Unlike the other commandments, which are prohibitive, the fourth commandment is both prescriptive and invitational. It invites us to embrace a rhythm of work and rest, reflecting God's love and care for us. By observing the Sabbath, we express our love for God, trust in His provision, and acknowledge the essential value of rest and worship in our lives.

The Origin of the Sabbath

The concept of the Sabbath has its roots in the creation narrative. In Genesis 2:2-3, we read, "And on the seventh day God finished the work that he had done, and he rested on the seventh day from all the work that he had done. So God blessed the seventh day and made it holy because on it God rested from all the work that he had done in creation." God's rest on the seventh day was not due to fatigue, but it was a divine cessation from creative activity, a celebration of the goodness of His creation.

God's rest serves as a model for humanity. Just as God rested, He called us to rest. The Sabbath is a reminder that we are not defined solely by our work and productivity. It is an acknowledgment of God as Creator and Sustainer, recognizing that our lives are ultimately in His hands.

The Gift of Rest

The Sabbath is a gift of rest from God. In a world that often glorifies busyness and constant activity, the Sabbath offers a countercultural rhythm of rest and renewal. It is a day set apart from the demands of daily life, a time to pause, reflect, and rejuvenate.

This rest is not merely physical but also spiritual and emotional. It allows us to step back from our routines and reconnect with God, ourselves, and our loved ones. The Sabbath provides space for worship, reflection, and gratitude, fostering a deeper sense of peace and well-being.

Trust in God's Provision

Observing the Sabbath is an act of trust in God's provision. It requires us to set aside our work and trust that God will take care of our needs. This can be especially challenging in a culture that equates productivity with worth and security.

The command to rest on the Sabbath teaches us that our value and security are not based on our efforts but on God's faithfulness. It reminds us that God is our provider and that He sustains us even when we are not working. By resting, we demonstrate our trust in God's provision and our reliance on His grace.

Acknowledging the Value of Rest and Worship

The fourth commandment highlights the intrinsic value of rest and worship. Rest is not a luxury or an indulgence but a necessary part of a balanced and healthy life. It allows us to recharge and refocus, enhancing our productivity and creativity during the other six days.

Worship is also central to the Sabbath. It is a time to honor and glorify God, to reflect on His goodness and grace. Worship on the Sabbath helps us to realign our priorities, putting God at the center of our lives. It fosters a spirit of gratitude and reverence, deepening our relationship with Him.

The Communal Aspect of the Sabbath

The commandment to observe the Sabbath extends beyond individual rest. It includes family members, servants, livestock, and even strangers within the community. This communal aspect underscores the social and relational dimensions of the Sabbath. It promotes a culture of rest and respect for all, regardless of status or role.

By ensuring that everyone within the community observes the Sabbath, the commandment fosters equality and compassion. It recognizes that rest is a fundamental human need and right, promoting a more just and caring society.

The Sabbath in the New Testament

In the New Testament, Jesus affirms the importance of the Sabbath but also redefines its purpose. He emphasizes that the Sabbath was made for humanity, not humanity for the Sabbath (Mark 2:27). Jesus' healing on the Sabbath and His teachings highlight that the Sabbath is a day for doing good, for restoring and renewing life.

Jesus' approach to the Sabbath underscores its role as a day of blessing and grace, rather than a burden. It is a time to experience God's love and to extend that love to others through acts of kindness and compassion.

Living Out the Fourth Commandment

Living out the fourth commandment involves intentional practices of rest and worship. This can be challenging in a culture that often values productivity over well-being. However, embracing the Sabbath requires us to prioritize our spiritual and emotional health, recognizing the importance of balance and renewal.

Practically, this might involve setting aside a specific day each week for rest and worship, free from work-related activities. It can include spending time in nature, engaging in reflective practices, participating in communal worship, and nurturing relationships with family and friends.

Moreover, living out the Sabbath calls us to advocate for rest and justice in our communities. This can involve supporting fair labor practices, promoting work-life balance, and ensuring that rest and renewal are accessible to all.

The Blessings of the Sabbath

Observing the Sabbath brings numerous blessings. It enhances our physical and mental health, reduces stress, and increases our sense of well-being. It fosters deeper relationships with God and others, creating a stronger sense of community and connection.

The Sabbath also enriches our spiritual lives. It provides regular opportunities for worship, reflection, and spiritual growth. It helps us to cultivate gratitude, reverence, and trust in God, deepening our faith and reliance on His grace.

The fourth commandment, "Remember the Sabbath day, to keep it holy," invites us to embrace a rhythm of rest and worship. It is a gift of rest that reflects God's love and care for us, a call to trust in His provision, and an acknowledgment of the value of rest and worship in our lives.

As we continue to explore the Ten Commandments, we see that each commandment is rooted in the theology of love. The fourth commandment teaches us about the importance of rest and worship as expressions of our love for God. May we respond to this call with hearts open to rest and renewal, trusting in God's provision and celebrating His goodness in our lives.

EXPOSITORY STUDY AND COMPREHENSIVE COMMENTARY VERSE 8

Verse 8:

"Remember the sabbath day, to keep it holy."

King James Bible's Reference:

"Remember the sabbath day, to keep it holy." (Exodus 20:8, KJV)

Interpretation:

This verse is part of the Ten Commandments, specifically the fourth commandment, which instructs the Israelites to observe the Sabbath day by keeping it holy. The command to "remember" suggests an ongoing, deliberate recognition of the Sabbath's significance.

Commentary:

"Remember the sabbath day": The command to remember implies that the Sabbath should be kept in the consciousness of the Israelites not only as a day of rest but also as a sign of the covenant between God and His people. It serves as a reminder of God's creation work, which He completed in six days and rested on the seventh (Genesis 2:2-3).

"To keep it holy": Keeping the Sabbath day holy means setting it apart from other days through rest and cessation of regular work. This sanctification of the day is a form of worship and acknowledgment of God's sovereignty and provision (Exodus 31:13-17).

Concordance:

- Remember the sabbath day: This phrase underscores the importance of not merely acknowledging the Sabbath but actively incorporating its observance into one's life as a perpetual covenant (Genesis 2:2-3; Deuteronomy 5:12-15).

- To keep it holy: This command indicates that the Sabbath should be distinguished from other days through special activities that honor God, like rest and refraining from secular labor (Exodus 31:13-17).

References from the King James Bible:

1. Genesis 2:2-3: "And on the seventh day God ended his work which he had made, and he rested on the seventh day from all his work which he had made. And God blessed the seventh day, and sanctified it: because that in it he had rested from all his work which God created and made."

2. Exodus 31:13-17: "Speak thou also unto the children of Israel, saying, Verily my sabbaths ye shall keep: for it is a sign between me and you throughout your generations; that ye may know that I am the Lord that doth sanctify you... It is a sign between me and the children of Israel forever: for in six days the Lord made heaven and earth, and on the seventh day he rested, and was refreshed."

3. Deuteronomy 5:12-15: "Keep the sabbath day to sanctify it, as the Lord thy God hath commanded thee. Six days thou shalt labour, and do all thy work: But the seventh

day is the sabbath of the Lord thy God: in it, thou shalt not do any work... And remember that thou wast a servant in the land of Egypt and that the Lord thy God brought thee out thence through a mighty hand and by a stretched out arm: therefore the Lord thy God commanded thee to keep the sabbath day."

Interpretation and Application:

- Rest and Reflection: The Sabbath provides an opportunity for rest and reflection, reminding believers of God's creation and His deliverance. It is a time to recharge physically and spiritually, reflecting on God's goodness and provision.

- Sign of Covenant: Observance of the Sabbath serves as a sign of the covenant between God and His people, symbolizing trust in God's provision and obedience to His commandments.

- Holiness and Separation: Keeping the Sabbath holy involves setting it apart from other days with a focus on spiritual activities and rest, emphasizing the distinction between the sacred and the secular.

Exploring further the implications of Exodus 20:8, particularly in terms of its relevance to modern spiritual practice and everyday life, offers a rich opportunity to connect ancient traditions with contemporary values and behaviors.

Spiritual Renewal and Rest

The commandment to "remember the Sabbath day, to keep it holy" underscores the importance of spiritual renewal and physical rest. In a modern context, this can be interpreted as setting aside regular periods for rest and reflection, away from the hustle of everyday work and responsibilities. This not only aligns with spiritual well-being but also supports mental and physical health.

Weekly Cycle of Rest

Adopting a weekly day of rest, regardless of religious affiliation, can help maintain a balanced lifestyle. For many, this could mean disconnecting from work emails and reducing screen time, engaging in recreational activities, or spending time in nature. This practice aligns with the Sabbath's original intent—to provide a break from labor and an opportunity to rejuvenate.

Community and Family Time

The Sabbath traditionally is a time for community gathering and family bonding. Modern applications could involve dedicating time each week to be with family or engage in community activities without the distractions of work tasks. This fosters stronger relationships and community ties, echoing the communal aspects of ancient Sabbath observances.

Reflection on Divinity and Creation

The original Sabbath commandment is deeply tied to the recognition of God's creation work. Today, this can translate into time spent in contemplation or meditation, acknowledging a higher power or the marvels of the natural world. For non-theistic perspectives, it could be a time to appreciate the interconnectedness of life and the environment.

Practical Observance

For those looking to integrate this commandment into their lives:

- Set clear boundaries for work and rest, ensuring that one day a week is work-free.

- Engage in restorative activities that differ from the usual weekday tasks—this could be anything from reading a book to taking a long walk or participating in a hobby.

- Connect with the community or family through shared meals, games, or service activities.

- Spend time in nature to reconnect with the environment, reflecting on the beauty and complexity of the natural world.

- Practice mindfulness or meditation to foster a deeper connection with oneself and, for believers, with God.

Challenges in Modern Society

Adopting a traditional Sabbath in modern times can be challenging, especially in societies that value constant productivity and connectivity. However, by reinterpreting the core principles of the Sabbath—rest, reflection, and renewal—individuals can find ways to incorporate these practices in a manner that respects their personal beliefs and lifestyle.

Cultural and Interfaith Perspectives

Understanding how the Sabbath is observed across different cultures and religions can also enrich one's own practice. For instance, exploring the Jewish Shabbat traditions, the Christian Sunday service, or rest practices in other religions can provide a broader perspective on the values of rest and communal engagement.

By revisiting and adapting the principles underlying Exodus 20:8, individuals can cultivate a rhythm of life that honors their need for rest, fosters community and family connections, and encourages spiritual or existential reflection.

CHAPTER 06

THE FIFTH COMMANDMENT: LOVE AND HONOR FOR PARENTS

"Honor your father and your mother, that your days may be long in the land that the Lord your God is giving you."

(Exodus 20:12)

The fifth commandment marks a transition from the commandments that focus on our relationship with God to those that govern our interactions with others. It underscores the importance of family and the respect and love owed to parents. This commandment establishes a framework for loving relationships within the family unit, promoting harmony and respect, and serves as a cornerstone for societal stability and well-being.

The Meaning of Honor

To honor someone means to show them respect, reverence, and esteem. In the context of the fifth commandment, honoring one's parents involves recognizing their role and authority within the family structure. It includes obedience, respect, and gratitude for the sacrifices they make and the care they provide.

Honoring parents is not limited to childhood obedience but extends throughout life. It involves caring for them in their old age, seeking their wisdom and guidance, and upholding their dignity. The commandment calls for a lifelong attitude of respect and appreciation.

The Importance of Family

The family is the fundamental building block of society. Strong, healthy family relationships contribute to the stability and flourishing of communities and nations. The fifth commandment emphasizes the vital role that parents play in nurturing, guiding, and supporting their children. It recognizes that respect and love within the family are essential for the well-being of individuals and society as a whole.

In honoring our parents, we acknowledge the sacrifices they make and the responsibilities they bear. Parenting involves significant emotional, physical, and financial investment. By showing respect and appreciation, children affirm the value of their parents' efforts and reinforce the importance of the family unit.

The Promise Attached to the Commandment

The fifth commandment is unique in that it comes with a promise: "that your days may be long in the land that the Lord your God is giving you." This promise highlights the benefits of honoring one's parents, both individually and collectively. A society that respects and cares for its elders is more likely to experience stability, longevity, and prosperity.

This promise can be understood in several ways. On a personal level, children who honor their parents are more likely to receive their guidance and wisdom, which can lead to a more fulfilling and successful life. On a societal level, communities that uphold family values and respect for elders are likely to experience greater cohesion, stability, and well-being.

The Broader Implications of the Commandment

While the fifth commandment specifically mentions parents, its principles extend to other relationships and authorities. Respect for parents can serve as a foundation for respecting other forms of authority, such as teachers, leaders, and elders. This broader respect contributes to social harmony and order.

Moreover, the commandment highlights the importance of intergenerational relationships. It encourages a culture where the wisdom and experience of older generations are valued and where younger generations learn to appreciate and honor their elders. This mutual respect fosters a sense of community and continuity.

Challenges to Honoring Parents

In contemporary society, honoring parents can sometimes be challenging. Cultural shifts, geographical mobility, and changing family dynamics can create distance and strain relationships. Additionally, not all parental relationships are healthy or supportive. In cases of abuse, neglect, or dysfunction, honoring parents can be complex and may require setting boundaries and seeking healing.

Despite these challenges, the principle of honoring parents remains relevant. It calls us to find ways to show respect and appreciation, even in difficult circumstances. This might involve seeking reconciliation, offering forgiveness, or finding other ways to honor their role in our lives while maintaining our well-being.

Honoring Parents in Practice

Honoring parents can take many forms, depending on individual circumstances and cultural contexts. Here are some practical ways to live out this commandment:

1. Respectful Communication: Speaking to and about parents with respect and courtesy. Avoiding harsh or dismissive language and expressing gratitude for their contributions.

2. Obedience and Support: Following their guidance and rules during childhood and offering support and assistance as they age. This can include helping with daily tasks, providing financial support, or simply spending time together.

3. Seeking Wisdom: Valuing their advice and experience. Consulting them on important decisions and acknowledging the value of their insights.

4. Caring for Their Needs: Ensuring that their physical, emotional, and social needs are met, especially as they grow older. This might involve arranging for medical care, helping with household tasks, or providing companionship.

5. Forgiveness and Reconciliation: Addressing past hurts and seeking to mend broken relationships. Offering forgiveness and seeking reconciliation where possible.

The Role of Parents

While the fifth commandment focuses on the child's responsibility to honor their parents, it also implies certain responsibilities for parents. To be worthy of honor, parents are called to provide love, guidance, and support. They are tasked with nurturing their children's physical, emotional, and spiritual well-being.

Parents are also called to model respect, integrity, and love. By living out these values, they create an environment where honor and respect can naturally flourish. The reciprocal nature of this commandment underscores the importance of mutual respect and love within the family.

The Spiritual Dimension of Honoring Parents

Honoring parents is not only a social and familial obligation but also a spiritual one. It reflects our relationship with God, who is often described as a loving parent. By honoring our earthly parents, we practice the principles of respect, gratitude, and love that are central to our faith.

Moreover, honoring parents can deepen our understanding of God's love and care for us. It provides a tangible way to express our faith and live out the values that God calls us to embody. This spiritual dimension adds depth and significance to the commandment, highlighting its role in our relationship with God and with others.

The fifth commandment, "Honor your father and your mother," underscores the importance of family and the respect and love owed to parents. It establishes a framework for loving relationships within the family unit, promoting harmony and respect. By honoring our parents, we acknowledge their role and sacrifices, contributing to the stability and well-being of our families and communities.

As we continue to explore the Ten Commandments, we see that each commandment is rooted in the theology of love. The fifth commandment teaches us about the importance of honoring and respecting those who have cared for us. May we respond to this call with hearts full of love and respect, fostering strong, healthy, and loving relationships within our families and communities?

EXPOSITORY STUDY AND COMPREHENSIVE COMMENTARY VERSE 12

Verse 12:

"Honour thy father and thy mother: that thy days may be long upon the land which the LORD thy God giveth thee."

King James Bible's Reference:

"Honour thy father and thy mother: that thy days may be long upon the land which the LORD thy God giveth thee." (Exodus 20:12, KJV)

Interpretation:

This verse presents the first commandment with a promise. It underscores the importance of respecting and valuing one's parents, which is foundational to societal stability and personal well-being. The commandment ties the honoring of one's parents to the promise of longevity and prosperity in the land provided by God.

Commentary:

"Honour thy father and thy mother": The term "honour" in this context involves respect, obedience, care, and upholding the dignity of one's parents. It encompasses a range of duties that reflect a reverential attitude toward parents and acknowledges their significant role in God's ordained authority structure within the family (Leviticus 19:3; Proverbs 1:8).

"That thy days may be long upon the land which the LORD thy God giveth thee": This part of the verse introduces a promise—longevity and a prosperous life in the Promised Land as a reward for obedience to this commandment. It suggests that societal stability and personal well-being are linked to how the younger generations treat their elders (Deuteronomy 5:16; Ephesians 6:2-3).

Concordance:

- Honour thy father and thy mother: This command reflects a universal principle emphasizing the foundational role of family in God's social order (Leviticus 19:3; Proverbs 1:8).

- That thy days may be long upon the land which the LORD thy God giveth thee: This phrase connects obedience to parental authority with tangible blessings, highlighting the reciprocal nature of God's covenant with His people (Deuteronomy 5:16; Ephesians 6:2-3).

References from the King James Bible:

1. Leviticus 19:3: "Ye shall fear every man his mother, and his father, and keep my sabbaths: I am the LORD your God."

2. Proverbs 1:8: "My son, hear the instruction of thy father, and forsake not the law of thy mother:"

3. Deuteronomy 5:16: "Honour thy father and thy mother, as the LORD thy God hath commanded thee; that thy days may be prolonged, and that it may go well with thee, in the land which the LORD thy God giveth thee."

4. Ephesians 6:2-3: "Honour thy father and mother; (which is the first commandment with promise;) That it may be well with thee, and thou mayest live long on the earth."

Interpretation and Application:

- Moral Foundation: Honouring one's parents is portrayed not merely as a duty but as a cornerstone of moral behavior that strengthens community bonds and ensures societal stability.

- Promise of Blessing: The promise of longevity and prosperity serves as a motivation for adherence to this commandment, teaching that God values and rewards those who respect and care for their parents.

- Cultural and Universal Principle: While the commandment was given to the Israelites, the principle of honoring parents is universal in its application, transcending cultural and temporal boundaries to form a basic tenet of social ethics.

Let's delve deeper into the theological implications and cultural applications of the commandment to "Honour thy father and thy mother," as stated in Exodus 20:12.

Theological Implications

1. Covenant Relationship:

- The commandment to honor one's parents is not isolated; it's part of the broader covenant between God and His people. This commandment underscores the idea that honoring authority figures, starting with parents, aligns with recognizing and honoring God's ultimate authority. This respect for authority reflects a well-ordered society in God's design, where familial relationships are foundational.

2. Moral Law and Grace:

- While the law, including the Ten Commandments, was given under the Old Covenant, the principle of honoring parents carries into the New Covenant under grace. It emphasizes that the moral law is enduring and continues to hold spiritual significance. Jesus Christ reiterated the importance of this commandment, thus affirming its unchanging value (Matthew 15:4).

3. Promise of Longevity:

- The promise of a long life and prosperity for honoring one's parents suggests a cause-and-effect relationship in divine blessings. Theologically, this reflects God's justice and providence, showing that He actively rewards obedience and right living, which are visible through blessings in one's life.

Cultural Applications

1. Family Structure and Social Stability:

- In many traditional societies, this commandment underpins the social structure, emphasizing strong family bonds and responsibilities across generations. Respecting and caring for elderly parents is seen not only as a moral duty but as a crucial part of societal stability and continuity.

2. Modern Implications:

- In contemporary contexts, where individualism often prevails over communal or familial obligations, this commandment challenges modern attitudes toward aging and care. It calls for a reevaluation of how modern societies care for the elderly and respect parental roles, suggesting that these are not merely personal choices but communal responsibilities with spiritual significance.

3. Inter-generational Relationships:

- The commandment fosters inter-generational respect and learning. In a culture where the old and the young increasingly lead segregated lives, this command emphasizes the importance of connection and mutual respect. It encourages younger generations to value the wisdom and experience of their elders, which can lead to richer, more integrated community life.

4. Legal and Ethical Considerations:

- This commandment also has implications for laws and policies related to family welfare and elder care. It suggests that societies benefit from policies that respect familial obligations and support the care of elderly parents, aligning with a biblical ethic that values the dignity and worth of every person across all stages of life.

The commandment to honor one's parents thus carries profound theological weight and practical relevance. It challenges individuals and societies to reflect on how they treat family members, particularly parents, in light of divine standards. It also underscores that such treatment has broader implications for personal well-being and societal health, bridging the gap between divine commandments and everyday living.

Would you like to explore any specific aspect further, perhaps how this commandment is viewed in different cultural contexts or its implications in modern legal systems?

CHAPTER 07

THE SIXTH COMMANDMENT: LOVE AND THE SANCTITY OF LIFE

"You shall not murder."

(Exodus 20:13)

The sixth commandment, "You shall not murder," is a brief yet profoundly significant directive. It underscores the sanctity of human life and reflects God's love for every individual. This commandment calls us to value and protect life, fostering a community where love and respect for life prevail. In this chapter, we will explore the deeper implications of this commandment and its relevance to our understanding of love and respect for human life.

The Sanctity of Human Life

The sixth commandment is grounded in the belief that human life is sacred. This sanctity is rooted in the creation narrative, where humans are made in the image of God (Genesis 1:27). This divine image bestows inherent dignity and worth upon every person, regardless of their circumstances or status.

Murder, the intentional taking of an innocent human life, is a direct affront to the image of God. It violates the fundamental principle that all life is precious and worthy of protection. By prohibiting murder, the sixth commandment affirms the value and dignity of each individual, recognizing that every life is a unique and irreplaceable gift from God.

Love as the Basis for the Prohibition

The prohibition against murder is intrinsically linked to the command to love our neighbors. In the New Testament, Jesus expands on the commandment, teaching that anger and hatred are akin to murder in God's eyes (Matthew 5:21-22). This connection highlights that the essence of the commandment is not merely the absence of violence but the presence of love and respect for others.

To love someone means to recognize their inherent worth and to seek their well-being. Murder, driven by hatred, jealousy, or malice, is the ultimate denial of this love. The sixth commandment, therefore, calls us to cultivate an attitude of love and respect for all people, ensuring that our actions reflect this fundamental respect for life.

The Broader Implications of the Commandment

While the commandment explicitly prohibits murder, its implications extend far beyond the act of taking a life. It encompasses any action or attitude that devalues human life or contributes to harm and suffering. This broader understanding calls us to:

1. Reject Violence and Harm: This includes physical violence, verbal abuse, and emotional harm. Any action that inflicts pain or diminishes the dignity of another person is contrary to the spirit of the commandment.

2. Promote Peace and Reconciliation: We are called to be peacemakers, actively seeking to resolve conflicts and restore broken relationships. This involves addressing the root causes of violence, such as injustice, inequality, and hatred.

3. Defend the Vulnerable: Protecting life means advocating for those who cannot defend themselves. This includes speaking out against injustice, supporting victims of violence, and working to create a society where all people are safe and valued.

4. Foster a Culture of Life: This involves promoting values and practices that uphold the sanctity of life. It includes supporting policies and initiatives that protect life, such as

healthcare, education, and social services that improve the quality of life for all.

The Role of Forgiveness and Reconciliation

In addressing the deeper issues of anger and hatred, Jesus calls us to a path of forgiveness and reconciliation. He teaches that harboring anger or resentment is destructive, both to ourselves and to others. Forgiveness is a crucial aspect of honoring the sanctity of life, as it breaks the cycle of violence and allows for healing and restoration.

Reconciliation goes beyond forgiveness. It involves restoring relationships and seeking justice in a way that respects the dignity of all parties involved. This process can be challenging, but it is essential for creating a community where love and respect for life prevail.

The Challenge of Modern Issues

The sixth commandment also invites us to consider contemporary issues that impact the sanctity of life. These include debates on topics such as abortion, euthanasia, capital punishment, and war. Each of these issues presents complex moral and ethical questions about the value and protection of human life.

Approaching these issues requires a commitment to the principles of love and respect for life. It involves careful consideration of the circumstances, the potential consequences, and the underlying values at stake. While opinions may differ, the commandment calls us to engage in these discussions with compassion, empathy, and a deep respect for the sanctity of life.

Living Out the Sixth Commandment

Living out the sixth commandment involves more than refraining from murder; it requires actively promoting a culture of life and respect. Here are some practical ways to embody this commandment:

1. Cultivate Compassion: Develop empathy and understanding for others. Seek to understand their experiences and challenges, and respond with kindness and support.

2. Promote Nonviolence: Advocate for peaceful solutions to conflicts and support initiatives that address the root causes of violence. Engage in community efforts that promote safety and well-being.

3. Support Life-Affirming Policies: Advocate for policies that protect and enhance human life, such as access to healthcare, education, and social services. Support efforts to address poverty, inequality, and other factors that undermine the sanctity of life.

4. Engage in Restorative Practices: In personal and community conflicts, seek restorative justice approaches that

focus on healing and reconciliation rather than retribution. Support initiatives that help individuals and communities recover from violence and trauma.

5. Educate and Raise Awareness: Educate yourself and others about the importance of the sanctity of life. Raise awareness about issues that threaten human life and dignity, and encourage others to take action.

The sixth commandment, "You shall not murder," is a powerful affirmation of the sanctity of human life. It reflects God's love for every individual and calls us to value and protect life in all its forms. By embracing this commandment, we commit to fostering a community where love, respect, and the protection of life prevail.

As we continue to explore the Ten Commandments, we see that each commandment is rooted in the theology of love. The sixth commandment teaches us about the profound value of human life and the importance of cultivating a culture of respect and care for all. May we respond to this call with hearts full of love and compassion, honoring the sanctity of life in all that we do.

EXPOSITORY STUDY AND COMPREHENSIVE COMMENTARY VERSE 13

Verse 13:

"Thou shalt not kill."

King James Bible's Reference:

"Thou shalt not kill." (Exodus 20:13, KJV)

Interpretation:

This verse is part of the Ten Commandments given by God to Moses on Mount Sinai. It succinctly prohibits the act of murder, emphasizing the sanctity of human life as a fundamental principle in both religious and ethical conduct.

Commentary:

"Thou shalt not kill": This commandment is straightforward in its directive, prohibiting the intentional taking of human life. The Hebrew word used here, רצח (ratsach), specifically refers to murder or unlawful killing, distinguishing it from killing in war or as capital punishment, which are addressed differently in the Hebrew Scriptures. This command reflects the value God places on human life, which is made in His image (Genesis 1:27; Genesis 9:6).

Concordance:

- Thou shalt not kill: This commandment emphasizes the prohibition against unlawfully taking a life, highlighting the sanctity and intrinsic value of human life which is a creation of God and made in His image (Genesis 1:27; Genesis 9:6).

References from the King James Bible:

1. Genesis 1:27: "So God created man in his own image, in the image of God created he him; male and female created he them."

2. Genesis 9:6: "Whoso sheddeth man's blood, by man shall his blood be shed: for in the image of God made he man."

Interpretation and Application:

- Sanctity of Life: The commandment underscores the sanctity of human life. It implies that life is a sacred gift from God and should be respected and protected. This principle forms the basis for many ethical and legal norms in both religious and secular contexts.

- Legal and Ethical Implications: "Thou shalt not kill" has profound legal and ethical implications. It serves as a foundational principle in criminal law regarding homicide and has been crucial in discussions about issues such as euthanasia, abortion, and capital punishment.

- Moral Responsibility: This commandment imposes a moral responsibility on individuals to respect others' lives. It calls for restraint and care in actions that could potentially harm others, promoting a society where life is valued and protected.

This commandment is a pivotal element in the moral teachings of not only Judaism but also Christianity and has influenced civil legislation and moral philosophy worldwide. It serves as a constant reminder of the value and dignity of human life.

Let's delve deeper into various aspects and implications of the commandment "Thou shalt not kill" (Exodus 20:13) from the Bible:

1. Theological Implications

- Image of God: Human beings are created in the image of God (Imago Dei), which is a foundational concept in Christian theology. This image imparts intrinsic value to every human life, making the act of murder not only a crime against another person but an affront to God Himself.

- Divine Sovereignty: The commandment reinforces the belief that life and death are under God's sovereign domain. Humans, therefore, are not to usurp what is God's prerogative.

2. Moral and Ethical Dimensions

- Sanctity of Life: This principle transcends cultural and religious boundaries, emphasizing that life is inherently valuable and should be protected. This impacts debates on euthanasia, suicide, abortion, and capital punishment, where the definitions of life and its ending are scrutinized.

- Moral Absolutism vs. Moral Relativism: The commandment suggests a moral absolute—murder is inherently wrong. This contrasts with moral relativism, where the morality of actions may depend on cultural or personal circumstances.

3. Legal and Societal Impact

- Criminal Law: The commandment forms the basis of laws against homicide in many societies. Legal systems differentiate between various types of homicide (e.g., murder, manslaughter), influenced by this fundamental command.

- War and Capital Punishment: The application of this commandment is complex in cases of war and capital punishment. Some interpretations allow for just wars and legal executions, while others call for complete non-violence, showing the diverse theological and ethical responses to the command.

4. Personal and Community Ethics

- Personal Responsibility: On a personal level, this command encourages individuals to consider their actions and their potential to harm others, promoting a culture of life and peace.

- Community Relationships: The commandment influences how communities handle justice and reconciliation. It encourages systems that value restoration over revenge.

5. Contemporary Issues

- Debates on Gun Control: In societies with high rates of gun violence, this commandment is often cited in debates over gun control as a moral argument for reducing access to firearms.

- Assisted Dying: The growing debate over assisted dying and euthanasia also sees this commandment used either as an argument for the sanctity of life or as a call for compassion, illustrating its complex application in modern ethical issues.

6. Historical and Cultural Context

- Historical Interpretations: Throughout history, interpretations of this commandment have evolved. Early Jewish and Christian interpretations often wrestled with reconciling this command with the realities of war and justice.

- Cultural Variations: Different cultures integrate the principle in various ways, influenced by local traditions, other religious beliefs, and historical contexts.

These aspects show the depth and breadth of the commandment's influence and its relevance to both personal behavior and broader societal norms. Would you like to focus on any specific area or related topic further?

CHAPTER 08

THE SEVENTH COMMANDMENT: LOVE AND MARITAL FAITHFULNESS

"You shall not commit adultery."

(Exodus 20:14)

The seventh commandment, "You shall not commit adultery," addresses the sanctity of marriage and the profound importance of marital fidelity. This commandment is not merely a prohibition against infidelity; it is a call to uphold the values of trust, loyalty, and love within the marital relationship. In this chapter, we will explore the deeper implications of this commandment and its relevance to our understanding of love and commitment in marriage.

The Sacredness of Marriage

Marriage is a sacred covenant established by God. From the beginning, God designed marriage to be a union between a man and a woman, characterized by mutual love, respect, and commitment. In Genesis 2:24, we read, "Therefore a man shall leave his father and his mother and hold fast to his wife, and they shall become one flesh." This verse highlights the intimate and exclusive nature of the marital relationship.

The seventh commandment protects the integrity of this sacred union. Adultery, which involves engaging in a sexual relationship outside of marriage, violates the trust and exclusivity that are foundational to marriage. It undermines the commitment and love that spouses pledge to each other, causing deep emotional and relational harm.

Love as the Basis for Marital Fidelity

At the heart of the prohibition against adultery is the principle of love. True marital fidelity is a profound expression of love and commitment. It involves honoring the vows made to one's spouse, maintaining trust and loyalty, and nurturing the emotional and physical bond that marriage entails.

Love in marriage is not merely a feeling but a deliberate choice and action. It involves prioritizing the well-being of one's spouse, being faithful in thought and deed, and working together to build a strong, healthy relationship. Marital fidelity reflects the depth of love and respect that spouses have for each other.

The Impact of Adultery

Adultery has far-reaching consequences that extend beyond the individuals directly involved. It can cause significant emotional pain, destroy trust, and lead to the breakdown of the marital relationship. The betrayal of adultery affects not only the spouses but also their families, friends, and communities.

The emotional wounds inflicted by adultery can be deep and long-lasting. Trust, once broken, is difficult to rebuild. The sense of betrayal and hurt can lead to feelings of anger, resentment, and insecurity. For many, the recovery from such a breach of trust requires significant time, effort, and often, professional support.

The Call to Purity and Integrity

The seventh commandment calls us to a life of purity and integrity. This extends beyond marital fidelity to encompass our thoughts, desires, and actions. Jesus, in His teachings, emphasized that adultery begins in the heart. In Matthew 5:27-28, He said, "You have heard that it was said, 'You shall not commit adultery.' But I say to you that everyone who looks at a woman with lustful intent has already committed adultery with her in his heart."

This teaching highlights the importance of guarding our hearts and minds against lustful thoughts and desires.

Purity involves more than refraining from physical acts of infidelity; it requires maintaining a mindset of respect and honor towards our spouse and others.

Building Strong Marital Relationships

Honoring the seventh commandment involves actively working to build and maintain strong marital relationships. Here are some practical ways to cultivate love, trust, and fidelity in marriage:

1. Open Communication: Maintain open, honest, and respectful communication with your spouse. Share your thoughts, feelings, and concerns, and listen actively to each other. Effective communication fosters understanding and strengthens the marital bond.

2. Quality Time: Spend quality time together, engaging in activities that you both enjoy. Regularly setting aside time to connect and nurture your relationship helps to reinforce your commitment and love.

3. Mutual Respect: Treat your spouse with respect and honor. Recognize and appreciate their contributions, strengths, and efforts. Mutual respect is foundational to a healthy and loving relationship.

4. Emotional Support: Be a source of emotional support for your spouse. Offer encouragement, empathy, and understanding, especially during challenging times. Providing

emotional support strengthens the marital bond and fosters a sense of security and trust.

5. Shared Values and Goals: Align your values and goals with your spouse. Working together towards common objectives and maintaining shared values helps to create a unified and purpose-driven relationship.

6. Faithfulness in Thought and Action: Guard against thoughts and actions that could undermine your marital fidelity. Avoid situations and behaviors that could lead to temptation or compromise your commitment to your spouse.

The Role of Forgiveness and Reconciliation

While the seventh commandment sets a high standard for marital fidelity, it also acknowledges the reality of human fallibility. In cases where adultery has occurred, the path to healing involves forgiveness and reconciliation. Forgiveness is a difficult but essential step in the healing process. It requires both the offender and the offended to seek healing and restoration.

Reconciliation involves rebuilding trust and working towards a renewed commitment. This process can be challenging and may require professional counseling and support. However, it is possible to restore and even strengthen the marital relationship through forgiveness and a commitment to change.

The Broader Implications of Marital Fidelity

Marital fidelity has broader implications for society. Strong, faithful marriages contribute to the stability and well-being of families and communities. They provide a foundation for raising children in a secure and loving environment and serve as a model of commitment and love for future generations.

Moreover, the principles of fidelity, trust, and commitment extend beyond marriage to other relationships. Upholding these values in our interactions with others fosters a culture of respect, integrity, and love.

The seventh commandment, "You shall not commit adultery," is a profound affirmation of the sanctity of marriage and the importance of marital fidelity. It reflects God's design for marriage as a covenant of love, trust, and commitment. By honoring this commandment, we uphold the values of love and respect that are essential for strong, healthy relationships.

As we continue to explore the Ten Commandments, we see that each commandment is rooted in the theology of love. The seventh commandment teaches us about the importance of faithfulness and integrity in our relationships. May we respond to this call with hearts full of love and commitment, nurturing our marriages and relationships in ways that honor God and reflect His love.

EXPOSITORY STUDY AND COMPREHENSIVE COMMENTARY VERSE 14

Verse 14:

"Thou shalt not commit adultery."

King James Bible's Reference:

"Thou shalt not commit adultery." (Exodus 20:14, KJV)

Interpretation:

This verse presents the seventh commandment from the Ten Commandments, which prohibits adultery. This commandment underscores the sanctity of marriage and the importance of fidelity within that covenant.

Commentary:

"Thou shalt not commit adultery": Adultery, in this context, refers to a sexual relationship where at least one of the participants is married to someone else. This commandment safeguards the integrity and unity of the marriage relationship, emphasizing the commitment that marriage entails (Matthew 5:27-28; Hebrews 13:4).

The prohibition of adultery highlights several key themes:

1. Sanctity of Marriage: Marriage is viewed as a sacred institution ordained by God. Adultery is seen as a severe violation of this sacred union.

2. Trust and Fidelity: Adultery breaches the trust upon which the marriage relationship is built. Fidelity is crucial for the stability and health of both the family and the broader community.

3. Moral and Social Stability: The commandment reflects God's concern for moral boundaries and social stability. By maintaining pure marriage relations, the community upholds a standard of morality that benefits everyone.

Concordance:

- Thou shalt not commit adultery: This phrase directly addresses the moral obligation to remain faithful to one's spouse, emphasizing the ethical demand placed upon individuals to honor their marital commitments (Matthew 5:27-28; Hebrews 13:4).

References from the King James Bible:

1. Matthew 5:27-28: "Ye have heard that it was said by them of old time, Thou shalt not commit adultery: But I say unto you, That whosoever looketh on a woman to lust after her hath committed adultery with her already in his heart."

2. Hebrews 13:4: "Marriage is honourable in all, and the bed undefiled: but whoremongers and adulterers God will judge."

Interpretation and Application:

- Ethical Integrity: The command to not commit adultery calls for individuals to maintain ethical integrity within their personal relationships, particularly within marriage. It challenges believers to uphold loyalty and faithfulness.

- Personal Discipline: This commandment also touches on the theme of personal discipline, particularly in controlling one's desires and impulses. Jesus expands on this commandment by addressing not only the physical act of adultery but also the intentions and thoughts that lead to it.

- Community Ethos: By adhering to this commandment, the community establishes a social ethos that values and respects the marital bond. It serves to protect families, reduce social strife, and promote a stable and healthy environment for raising children.

The prohibition against adultery is fundamental in fostering trust, respect, and fidelity in personal relationships and is crucial for the overall moral and social fabric of the community.

Exploring the commandment "Thou shalt not commit adultery" further, we can delve into its broader implications for personal conduct, societal norms, and spiritual principles as they are developed throughout the Bible.

1. Broader Personal and Spiritual Implications

Spiritual Fidelity: In the Bible, the relationship between God and His people is often depicted as a marriage. Idolatry is frequently described as spiritual adultery, illustrating the seriousness of being unfaithful to God by pursuing other gods or idols. This metaphor deepens the understanding of adultery, extending it from a physical act to a spiritual betrayal (Hosea 1-3; James 4:4).

Integrity and Honesty: The commandment not only promotes physical fidelity but also calls for integrity in one's thoughts and intentions. Jesus emphasizes this in the Sermon on the Mount, where He expands the definition of adultery to include lustful thoughts, thus addressing the root of the sin before it manifests in action (Matthew 5:27-28).

2. Societal Impact and Norms

Protecting Family Structure: Adultery can lead to broken families and damaged relationships which have a ripple effect across society. By upholding this commandment, the community works towards maintaining family integrity, providing a stable environment for raising children, and minimizing emotional and psychological harm.

Legal and Social Repercussions: In ancient Israel, adultery was not only a moral failing but also a legal offense that carried severe penalties. This underscores the gravity of the act and its potential to disrupt social order (Leviticus 20:10). In modern times, while the legal penalties may differ, the social repercussions still include loss of trust and respect.

3. Theological Dimensions

Divine Justice and Mercy: The narratives and laws surrounding adultery in the Bible also showcase God's attributes of justice and mercy. While adultery is met with strict judgments, there are also profound instances of forgiveness and restoration, illustrating God's willingness to forgive and restore those who repent (John 8:1-11).

Covenant Theology: Adultery as a violation of a covenant mirrors the larger Biblical theme of covenant between God and His people. Just as marital fidelity symbolizes trust and commitment, the spiritual covenant emphasizes faithfulness to God's laws and His reciprocal commitment to His people.

4. Practical Applications

Counseling and Support: Understanding the deep harm caused by adultery can guide pastoral care and counseling efforts within communities. Support systems and counseling are vital for helping those affected by adultery to heal, rebuild trust, and possibly restore relationships.

Education and Prevention: Teaching about the sanctity of marriage and the importance of fidelity from a young age can help prevent adultery. Educational efforts can focus on developing strong moral foundations and understanding the profound impacts of our actions on others.

The commandment "Thou shalt not commit adultery" encompasses a wide range of moral, spiritual, and societal teachings. It calls for a deep commitment to fidelity in all relationships, reflecting the broader Biblical principles of love, respect, and covenantal faithfulness. This commandment challenges believers to live lives of integrity, not just in action but in thought and spirit, aligning themselves with the divine will and fostering a just and compassionate society.

CHAPTER 09

THE EIGHTH COMMANDMENT: LOVE AND RESPECT FOR OTHERS' PROPERTY

"You shall not steal."

(Exodus 20:15)

The eighth commandment, "You shall not steal," addresses the ethical and moral obligation to respect the property and possessions of others. This commandment extends beyond the simple act of theft; it encompasses the broader principles of honesty, integrity, and respect for others' rights and dignity. Respecting others' property is an act of love and consideration that fosters a community based on trust and mutual respect.

The Principle of Ownership

The concept of ownership is foundational to the eighth commandment. Ownership implies that individuals have the right to possess, use, and enjoy their property without fear of unjust deprivation. This principle is rooted in the understanding that God is the ultimate owner of all things, and He entrusts us with stewardship over certain resources and possessions.

By prohibiting theft, the eighth commandment affirms the right of individuals to own property and the responsibility of others to respect that right. This respect for ownership is essential for maintaining social order and fostering a sense of security and trust within the community.

Love as the Basis for Respecting Property

At the heart of the eighth commandment is the principle of love. Respecting others' property is an expression of love and consideration for their well-being. It acknowledges the effort and resources invested in acquiring and maintaining possessions and recognizes the impact that theft can have on an individual's life.

When we love our neighbors, we seek to uphold their rights and dignity. This includes honoring their right to own and enjoy their property. Theft, in any form, is a violation of this love and respect, causing harm and undermining trust within the community.

The Broader Implications of Stealing

While the commandment explicitly addresses theft, its implications extend to various forms of dishonesty and exploitation. These include:

1. Fraud and Deception: Engaging in dishonest practices, such as fraud or deception, to gain an unfair advantage or benefit at the expense of others.

2. Cheating and Exploitation: Taking advantage of others through unfair practices, such as underpaying employees, overcharging customers, or exploiting vulnerable individuals.

3. Negligence and Waste: Failing to fulfill responsibilities or misusing resources entrusted to us, thereby depriving others of their rightful benefits.

4. Intellectual Property Theft: Stealing ideas, creations, or inventions without proper acknowledgment or compensation.

Each of these forms of theft undermines trust and respect within the community, causing harm and injustice. The eighth commandment calls us to uphold honesty and integrity in all our dealings, ensuring that we do not deprive others of their rightful possessions or benefits.

The Role of Contentment and Gratitude

Contentment and gratitude play a crucial role in upholding the eighth commandment. Discontentment and envy often drive individuals to steal or engage in dishonest practices. Cultivating a heart of contentment and gratitude helps us appreciate what we have and resist the temptation to take what belongs to others.

The apostle Paul, in his letter to the Philippians, writes, "I have learned in whatever situation I am to be content" (Philippians 4:11). This attitude of contentment enables us to respect the property and possessions of others, recognizing that true satisfaction and fulfillment come from our relationship with God rather than material wealth.

Building a Community Based on Trust

Respecting others' property is essential for building a community based on trust and mutual respect. Trust is a foundational element of healthy relationships and social interactions. When individuals respect each other's property rights, they contribute to a culture of trust and security, where people feel safe and valued.

A community based on trust fosters cooperation, collaboration, and mutual support. It encourages individuals to contribute positively to society, knowing that their rights and possessions will be respected. This, in turn, promotes social harmony and well-being.

The Call to Generosity and Stewardship

While the eighth commandment calls us to respect others' property, it also invites us to practice generosity and stewardship. As stewards of the resources and possessions entrusted to us, we are called to use them responsibly and for the benefit of others.

Generosity involves sharing our resources with those in need, and recognizing that everything we have ultimately belongs to God. By practicing generosity, we reflect God's love and compassion, contributing to the well-being of others and the flourishing of the community.

Addressing Economic Injustice

The eighth commandment also calls us to address economic injustice and inequality. Theft can sometimes be driven by systemic issues, such as poverty, unemployment, and lack of access to resources. Addressing these root causes requires a commitment to justice and equity, ensuring that all individuals have the opportunity to thrive.

This may involve advocating for fair wages, supporting initiatives that provide access to education and employment, and working to create an economic system that promotes justice and dignity for all. By addressing economic injustice, we help create a society where the principles of the eighth commandment can be upheld.

Living Out the Eighth Commandment

Living out the eighth commandment involves cultivating a lifestyle of honesty, integrity, and respect for others' property. Here are some practical ways to embody this commandment:

1. Honest Practices: Commit to honesty in all your dealings, whether in business, personal relationships, or daily interactions. Avoid any form of deceit or exploitation.

2. Respect for Property: Respect the property and possessions of others, recognizing their rights and dignity. This includes avoiding any form of theft, vandalism, or misuse of others' belongings.

3. Contentment and Gratitude: Cultivate a heart of contentment and gratitude, appreciating what you have and resisting the temptation to take what belongs to others.

4. Generosity and Stewardship: Practice generosity by sharing your resources with those in need and using your possessions responsibly and for the benefit of others.

5. Advocacy for Justice: Advocate for economic justice and equity, working to address the root causes of theft and economic exploitation. Support initiatives that promote fair wages, access to resources, and opportunities for all.

The eighth commandment, "You shall not steal," calls us to respect the property and possessions of others as an expression of love and consideration. It acknowledges the rights and dignity of individuals, fostering a community based on trust and mutual respect. By upholding this commandment, we contribute to the well-being and flourishing of our communities.

As we continue to explore the Ten Commandments, we see that each commandment is rooted in the theology of love. The eighth commandment teaches us about the importance of honesty, integrity, and respect for others. May we respond to this call with hearts full of love and respect, living out the principles of the eighth commandment in our daily lives and contributing to a culture of trust and mutual support?

EXPOSITORY STUDY AND COMPREHENSIVE COMMENTARY VERSE 15

Verse 15:

"Thou shalt not steal."

King James Bible's Reference:

"Thou shalt not steal." (Exodus 20:15, KJV)

Interpretation:

This verse is part of the Ten Commandments, which God gave to Moses on Mount Sinai. The commandment "Thou shalt not steal" is a universal principle against taking something that does not rightfully belong to one without permission. It emphasizes respect for the property rights of others and is foundational to the social and moral order.

Commentary:

"Thou shalt not steal": This commandment addresses the unlawful taking of property belonging to another, encompassing theft of any kind—whether small or large, covert or overt. It implies a broader ethical framework that values honesty, integrity, and justice, and is integral to the maintenance of trust and fairness within a community (Leviticus 19:11; Ephesians 4:28).

The prohibition against stealing recognizes the value and sanctity of personal and communal possessions. In a wider biblical context, this commandment also points towards a respect for the rights and dignity of others, discouraging not only the act of theft but also covetousness, which often leads to theft (Exodus 20:17; Matthew 19:18).

Concordance:

- Thou shalt not steal: This phrase underscores a fundamental moral law that is vital for the functioning of any society and is reiterated throughout the Bible as a cornerstone of ethical behavior (Leviticus 19:11; Ephesians 4:28).

References from the King James Bible:

1. Leviticus 19:11: "Ye shall not steal, neither deal falsely, neither lie one to another."

2. Ephesians 4:28: "Let him that stole steal no more: but rather let him labour, working with his hands the thing which is good, that he may have to give to him that needeth."

3. Exodus 20:17: "Thou shalt not covet thy neighbour's house, thou shalt not covet thy neighbour's wife, nor his manservant, nor his maidservant, nor his ox, nor his ass, nor any thing that is thy neighbour's."

4. Matthew 19:18: "He saith unto him, Which? Jesus said, Thou shalt do no murder, Thou shalt not commit adultery, Thou shalt not steal, Thou shalt not bear false witness,"

Interpretation and Application:

- Moral and Social Order: The commandment to not steal is essential for maintaining moral and social order. It encourages individuals to respect others' property and promotes a society where trust and justice prevail.

- Ethical Living: This commandment calls for ethical living and personal integrity. It encourages individuals to seek lawful means of acquiring what they need or desire, fostering a culture of honesty and hard work.

- Protection of Property: The commandment protects personal and communal property, ensuring that all have the security and peace of mind to enjoy the fruits of their labor without fear of unjust loss.

- Spiritual Integrity: On a spiritual level, this commandment teaches restraint and contentment, guiding believers to trust in God's provision rather than taking unjustly from others.

Let's delve deeper into the implications and broader applications of the commandment "Thou shalt not steal" from Exodus 20:15, exploring its spiritual, social, and ethical dimensions.

Spiritual Implications

Cultivating Contentment: The commandment against stealing is fundamentally about cultivating a spirit of contentment and trust in God's provision. In a spiritual context, this commandment challenges individuals to rely on God rather than succumbing to the temptation to unlawfully take what belongs to others. This reflects a deeper trust in God's timing and provision (Philippians 4:12-13).

Respect for Divine Ownership: From a theological standpoint, recognizing that ultimately all things belong to God helps believers understand that theft is not just against another person but against God's sovereign order. This acknowledgment promotes a deeper respect for the sanctity of what God has entrusted to others (Psalm 24:1).

Social Implications

Building Trust: In societal terms, adherence to this commandment is crucial for building trust among community members. When people respect each other's property rights, it creates a stable environment where individuals and businesses can thrive without fear of exploitation or theft (Proverbs 22:1).

Promoting Social Justice: The commandment against stealing is also closely linked to social justice. By respecting the possessions of others, society acknowledges the importance of equitable distribution of resources and the right of individuals to retain the fruits of their labor. This can also extend to advocating against forms of systemic theft, such as unfair wages, exploitative labor practices, and corruption (James 5:4).

Ethical Implications

Ethical Consumption: In modern contexts, this commandment can be applied to ethical consumption practices. It calls for individuals to consider the origins of what they buy and use, ensuring that their consumption does not indirectly support the theft of labor, resources, or livelihood (1 Timothy 6:10).

Integrity in Business: For businesses, adhering to this commandment means engaging in fair trade practices, avoiding plagiarism, respecting intellectual property rights, and maintaining transparency in transactions to ensure that no form of deceit or theft occurs (Leviticus 19:35-36).

Practical Applications

Education and Awareness: Teaching about the implications of stealing and promoting awareness about the broader impact of theft can help cultivate a culture of honesty and integrity from a young age. Schools, religious institutions, and families play critical roles in instilling these values.

Restorative Justice: When theft occurs, promoting principles of restorative justice can help repair the harm caused by theft. This involves the offender making amends, which may include restitution or other forms of reconciliation with the victim.

Community Involvement: Communities can strengthen adherence to this commandment by creating support systems that provide for the needs of their members, reducing the temptation to steal. Community programs, local charities, and social services play vital roles in providing safety nets.

These diverse applications and implications highlight the commandment's relevance across various aspects of life, reinforcing its enduring importance in promoting a just, ethical, and spiritually aligned society.

Would you like to explore any specific area further or discuss how this commandment intersects with contemporary issues?

CHAPTER 10

THE NINTH COMMANDMENT: LOVE AND TRUTHFULNESS

"You shall not bear false witness against your neighbor."

(Exodus 20:16)

The ninth commandment, "You shall not bear false witness against your neighbor," emphasizes the crucial role of truthfulness in fostering loving relationships and a just society. This commandment addresses the importance of honesty and integrity, which are essential for building trust and maintaining healthy, loving relationships within any community. In this chapter, we will explore the deeper implications of this commandment and its relevance to our understanding of love and truth.

The Importance of Truthfulness

Truthfulness is a fundamental aspect of moral and ethical behavior. It involves being honest in our words, actions, and intentions. Truthfulness is not only about avoiding lies but also about promoting transparency, integrity, and trustworthiness. In a world where deception and dishonesty can cause significant harm, the ninth commandment calls us to uphold the truth in all our interactions.

Truthfulness is essential for building trust, which is the foundation of any healthy relationship. Without trust, relationships cannot flourish, and communities cannot thrive. Honesty fosters mutual respect, understanding, and cooperation, creating an environment where love and justice can prevail.

The Harm of Bearing False Witness

Bearing false witness, or lying, can take many forms, including slander, gossip, false accusations, and deceit. Each of these actions undermines trust and can cause significant harm to individuals and communities. The ninth commandment specifically addresses the act of giving false testimony, particularly in a legal context, where lying can lead to unjust outcomes and the persecution of innocent individuals.

The harm caused by false witnesses extends beyond the immediate victim. It erodes the integrity of the community, damages reputations, and creates an atmosphere of suspicion and distrust. When truth is compromised, justice is undermined, and the fabric of society begins to fray.

Love as the Basis for Truthfulness

At the heart of the ninth commandment is the principle of love. Truthfulness is an expression of love and respect for others. When we speak the truth, we honor the dignity and worth of those around us. We demonstrate our commitment to justice and our desire to build healthy, trusting relationships.

Love and truth are inseparable. In 1 Corinthians 13:6, the apostle Paul writes, "Love does not delight in evil but rejoices with the truth." True love seeks the best for others, and this includes being honest and transparent in our dealings. Deception and dishonesty are antithetical to love, as they harm and exploit others for personal gain.

The Broader Implications of Truthfulness

While the commandment explicitly addresses false testimony, its implications extend to all forms of dishonesty and deceit. These include:

1. Gossip and Slander: Spreading rumors or making false statements about others, which can damage reputations and relationships.

2. Deception and Fraud: Engaging in deceitful practices to gain an unfair advantage or benefit at the expense of others.

3. Hypocrisy: Presenting a false image of oneself, pretending to be something one is not, or hiding one's true intentions.

4. False Promises: Making commitments or promises without the intention of keeping them.

Each of these forms of dishonesty undermines trust and respect within the community. The ninth commandment calls us to uphold truthfulness in all aspects of our lives, ensuring that our words and actions align with our values and commitments.

The Role of Integrity

Integrity is the quality of being honest and having strong moral principles. It involves consistency between our beliefs, words, and actions. Integrity is essential for living out the ninth commandment, as it requires us to be truthful not only in our speech but also in our behavior.

Living with integrity means being trustworthy and reliable. It means standing by the truth, even when it is difficult or inconvenient. It involves being transparent and accountable, ensuring that our actions reflect our commitment to honesty and justice.

The Challenge of Speaking the Truth in Love

While truthfulness is essential, it must be balanced with sensitivity and compassion. Speaking the truth in love involves being honest while also considering the impact of our words on others. It requires wisdom and discernment to know when and how to speak the truth in a way that is constructive and caring.

In Ephesians 4:15, Paul encourages believers to "speak the truth in love." This means being honest and straightforward, but also gentle and kind. It involves addressing difficult issues with empathy and understanding, seeking to build up rather than tear down.

The Call to Transparency and Accountability

The ninth commandment also calls for transparency and accountability in our personal and communal lives. Transparency involves being open and honest about our actions, decisions, and intentions. It fosters trust and prevents misunderstandings and conflicts.

Accountability means taking responsibility for our words and actions. It involves admitting when we are wrong and making amends for any harm caused. By being accountable, we demonstrate our commitment to truth and integrity, reinforcing trust within the community.

Living Out the Ninth Commandment

Living out the ninth commandment involves cultivating a lifestyle of honesty, integrity, and respect for others. Here are some practical ways to embody this commandment:

1. Honest Communication: Commit to being honest in all your interactions. Avoid deceit, exaggeration, and falsehood, and strive to speak the truth with clarity and compassion.

2. Avoid Gossip and Slander: Refrain from spreading rumors or making false statements about others. Focus on uplifting and encouraging others rather than tearing them down.

3. Transparency and Accountability: Be open and honest about your actions and decisions. Take responsibility for your mistakes and work to make amends when necessary.

4. Consistent Integrity: Ensure that your words and actions align with your values and commitments. Live with integrity, being consistent in your beliefs and behavior.

5. Encourage Truthfulness: Promote a culture of honesty and integrity within your community. Encourage others to speak the truth and hold each other accountable.

The Blessings of Truthfulness

Upholding the ninth commandment brings numerous blessings. Truthfulness fosters trust and respect within relationships, creating a strong foundation for love and cooperation. It promotes justice and fairness, ensuring that individuals are treated with dignity and respect.

Living with integrity and honesty also brings personal fulfillment and peace of mind. It frees us from the burden of deceit and the fear of being exposed. By embracing truthfulness, we align ourselves with God's character and reflect His love and righteousness in our lives.

The ninth commandment, "You shall not bear false witness against your neighbor," calls us to uphold truthfulness as a cornerstone of loving relationships and a just society. It emphasizes the importance of honesty, integrity, and respect for others, fostering a community based on trust and mutual respect.

As we continue to explore the Ten Commandments, we see that each commandment is rooted in the theology of love. The ninth commandment teaches us about the essential role of truthfulness in our relationships and communities. May we respond to this call with hearts full of love and integrity, living out the principles of the ninth commandment in our daily lives and contributing to a culture of honesty and trust.

EXPOSITORY STUDY AND COMPREHENSIVE COMMENTARY VERSE 16

Verse 16:

"Thou shalt not bear false witness against thy neighbour."

King James Bible's Reference:

"Thou shalt not bear false witness against thy neighbour." (Exodus 20:16, KJV)

Interpretation:

This verse is the ninth commandment among the Ten Commandments given by God to Moses on Mount Sinai. It prohibits lying or giving false testimony against another person. This commandment underscores the importance of truthfulness and integrity in the community.

Commentary:

"Thou shalt not bear false witness against thy neighbour": This commandment forbids lying about others, particularly in legal proceedings or situations where the truth is essential for justice. Bearing false witness can harm individuals and corrupt the community's moral and social fabric. The term "neighbour" in this context refers to others within the community, emphasizing the relational aspect of the commandment.

This commandment not only promotes truthfulness but also protects individuals from slander, libel, and false accusations. It is fundamental for maintaining justice and fairness within society (Proverbs 6:16-19; Deuteronomy 19:18-19).

Concordance:

- Thou shalt not bear false witness against thy neighbour: This phrase directly commands the avoidance of falsehood in dealings with others, especially in matters where one's testimony might influence the life and well-being of another person (Proverbs 6:16-19; Deuteronomy 19:18-19).

References from the King James Bible:

1. Proverbs 6:16-19: "These six things doth the LORD hate: yea, seven are an abomination unto him: A proud look, a lying tongue, and hands that shed innocent blood, An heart that deviseth wicked imaginations, feet that be swift in running to mischief, A false witness that speaketh lies, and he that soweth discord among brethren."

2. Deuteronomy 19:18-19: "And the judges shall make diligent inquisition: and, behold, if the witness be a false witness, and hath testified falsely against his brother; Then

shall ye do unto him, as he had thought to have done unto his brother: so shalt thou put the evil away from among you."

Interpretation and Application:

- Promotion of Truth and Justice: This commandment is foundational for promoting a culture of truth and justice in society. It helps ensure that justice is based on truth and that individuals are protected from false accusations.

- Moral Integrity: The prohibition against bearing false witness calls for moral integrity in personal and public life. It requires individuals to be truthful in their statements and actions, especially when these might impact others.

- Social Harmony: By discouraging falsehood, this commandment promotes social harmony and trust within the community. It supports the creation of a community where people can rely on the truthfulness and reliability of others, which is crucial for cooperative living and social stability.

This commandment, integral to the legal and moral framework of many societies, highlights the enduring relevance of biblical laws in fostering ethical behavior and societal well-being.

Let's delve deeper into the implications and broader context of the commandment "Thou shalt not bear false witness against thy neighbour" found in Exodus 20:16.

Historical and Cultural Context

In ancient Israel, the judicial system relied heavily on oral testimony because there were no forensic technologies like today. The testimony of witnesses was crucial in determining the outcome of legal disputes and criminal cases. The ninth commandment served as a critical safeguard against judicial errors and miscarriages of justice, emphasizing the importance of integrity in legal proceedings.

Ethical and Moral Implications

1. Truth in Society: This commandment underscores the value of truth as foundational to the function of any society. A culture that disregards truth is prone to corruption and injustice. By instilling this command as a divine law, it was intended to create a community where honesty is held in high regard.

2. Personal Integrity: Beyond legal settings, this commandment is a call to personal integrity. It encourages individuals to live lives characterized by honesty and sincerity in all interactions, not just in giving legal testimony. This builds trust and strengthens relationships within the community.

3. Prevention of Harm: False testimony can lead to innocent people being punished or the guilty being acquitted, both of which have severe societal repercussions. This

commandment helps prevent such harm by establishing the seriousness of false accusations.

Theological Implications

1. God's Nature: The command reflects God's nature—He is a God of truth (Psalm 31:5). By calling His people to truthfulness, God invites them to reflect His character in their lives.

2. Sin and Its Consequences: The Bible often discusses the destructive power of sin, not just in individual lives but within the community. Bearing false witness is a sin that can tear apart the fabric of community life, leading to mistrust and fear.

3. Redemption and Forgiveness: While the Law prescribes high standards, it is coupled with the themes of redemption and forgiveness throughout the Bible. Even those who fail to live up to these standards can find forgiveness and a new start through repentance and God's grace.

Modern Applications

1. In the Workplace: This commandment can be applied to maintaining honesty in professional environments, avoiding slander, and not taking credit for others' work.

2. In the Media: In an age of misinformation, this commandment challenges both consumers and creators of

media to prioritize truth and accuracy over sensationalism or personal bias.

3. Social Media Conduct: It also speaks to the integrity required in our digital interactions, emphasizing the need to be truthful and kind in our communications on social media platforms, where false information can easily be spread.

Broader Biblical References

- Proverbs 12:22: "Lying lips are an abomination to the LORD: but they that deal truly are his delight."

- Matthew 12:36-37: "But I say unto you, That every idle word that men shall speak, they shall give account thereof in the day of judgment. For by thy words, thou shalt be justified, and by thy words thou shalt be condemned."

This deeper exploration reveals that the commandment "Thou shalt not bear false witness" extends far beyond the courtroom; it is about fostering a culture of truth and integrity that mirrors the character of God. It remains profoundly relevant today, challenging us to evaluate how we embody truth in our daily lives. If you have specific aspects or applications you'd like to explore further, feel free to ask!

CHAPTER 11

THE TENTH COMMANDMENT: LOVE AND CONTENTMENT

"You shall not covet your neighbor's house; you shall not covet your neighbor's wife, or his male servant, or his female servant, or his ox, or his donkey, or anything that is your neighbor's."

(Exodus 20:17)

The tenth commandment, "You shall not covet," addresses the inner attitudes and desires of the heart. It calls us to cultivate contentment and gratitude, steering clear of envy and greed. This commandment is unique among the Ten Commandments because it focuses not on external actions but on internal dispositions. By fostering a heart of contentment, we can avoid the destructive nature of covetousness and embrace a life of love and gratitude.

Understanding Covetousness

To covet means to have an intense desire for something that belongs to someone else. It goes beyond mere admiration or aspiration; it involves a longing that can lead to resentment, envy, and dissatisfaction. Covetousness often manifests in thoughts and feelings of discontent, jealousy, and an insatiable craving for more.

The commandment specifically lists examples of what one should not covet, including a neighbor's house, spouse, servants, and animals. These examples highlight that covetousness can pertain to material possessions, relationships, and status. The underlying message is clear: desiring what belongs to others disrupts our peace and undermines our capacity to love and appreciate what we have.

The Destructive Nature of Covetousness

Covetousness is destructive because it breeds dissatisfaction and disrupts relationships. When we covet, we focus on what we lack rather than what we have, leading to a perpetual state of discontent. This dissatisfaction can drive us to make unwise decisions, harm others, and compromise our integrity in the pursuit of what we desire.

Moreover, covetousness can strain relationships. Envy and jealousy create barriers between us and others, fostering resentment and competition rather than love and cooperation. Coveting what belongs to our neighbor undermines trust and erodes the foundation of community and mutual respect.

Contentment as an Expression of Love

Contentment is the antidote to covetousness. It reflects a heart at peace, satisfied with what one has, and free from the insatiable desire for more. Contentment is an expression of love because it enables us to appreciate and cherish what we have and to celebrate the blessings of others without resentment.

The apostle Paul, in his letter to the Philippians, writes about the secret of contentment: "I have learned in whatever situation I am to be content" (Philippians 4:11). This contentment comes from a deep trust in God's provision and recognition that true fulfillment is found in our relationship with Him, not in material possessions or status.

Cultivating Contentment and Gratitude

Cultivating contentment involves developing a mindset of gratitude and appreciation. Here are some practical ways to foster contentment in our lives:

1. Practice Gratitude: Regularly take time to reflect on and give thanks for the blessings in your life. Keep a gratitude journal to record things you are thankful for each day. Focusing on what you have, rather than what you lack, can shift your perspective and increase your contentment.

2. Simplicity and Moderation: Embrace a lifestyle of simplicity and moderation. Avoid the constant pursuit of more and find joy in the simple pleasures of life. This can help reduce the temptation to covet and promote a sense of satisfaction with what you have.

3. Celebrate Others' Blessings: Learn to rejoice in the blessings and successes of others. Instead of feeling envious, celebrate with them and be genuinely happy for their good fortune. This can strengthen relationships and foster a sense of community and support.

4. Trust in God's Provision: Develop a deep trust in God's provision and care. Believe that He knows what you need and that He will provide for you in His perfect timing. Trusting in God can help alleviate anxiety and discontent.

5. Focus on Relationships: Prioritize relationships over material possessions. Invest in meaningful connections with family, friends, and community. These relationships provide lasting fulfillment and joy that material possessions cannot offer.

The Spiritual Dimension of Contentment

Contentment has a profound spiritual dimension. It involves recognizing that our ultimate fulfillment and satisfaction come from our relationship with God. Material possessions and status are temporary and can never fully satisfy the deep longings of our hearts. True contentment is found in knowing and trusting God, who is the source of all good things.

In 1 Timothy 6:6-7, Paul writes, "But godliness with contentment is great gain, for we brought nothing into the world, and we cannot take anything out of the world." This perspective helps us to focus on what truly matters and to cultivate a heart of contentment and gratitude.

Avoiding the Pitfalls of Consumerism

In our modern society, consumerism often fuels covetousness. The constant barrage of advertisements and societal pressure to acquire more can create a sense of inadequacy and dissatisfaction. To counteract this, we must be intentional about our attitudes towards possessions and wealth.

Practicing contentment involves recognizing the difference between needs and wants, and making conscious choices to resist the pull of consumerism. It means finding joy in what we have and valuing experiences and relationships over material goods. By doing so, we can avoid the pitfalls of consumerism and cultivate a heart of contentment.

Living Out the Tenth Commandment

Living out the tenth commandment involves cultivating a lifestyle of contentment, gratitude, and love. Here are some practical ways to embody this commandment:

1. Reflect on Your Desires: Regularly examine your desires and motivations. Ask yourself whether they are driven by contentment and gratitude or by envy and discontent. Adjust your attitudes and actions accordingly.

2. Simplify Your Life: Simplify your possessions and commitments. Focus on what truly matters and let go of excess. This can help reduce the temptation to covet and increase your sense of contentment.

3. Invest in Relationships: Prioritize relationships over material possessions. Spend time with loved ones, build meaningful connections, and invest in your community. These relationships provide lasting fulfillment and joy.

4. Cultivate Gratitude: Develop a practice of gratitude. Regularly take time to reflect on and give thanks for the blessings in your life. This can help shift your focus from what you lack to what you have.

5. Trust in God's Provision: Trust in God's provision and care. Believe that He knows what you need and that He will provide for you in His perfect timing. This trust can help alleviate anxiety and discontent.

The tenth commandment, "You shall not covet," calls us to cultivate a heart of contentment and gratitude. It reflects a life free from envy and greed, focusing instead on appreciating what we have and celebrating the blessings of others. By embracing this commandment, we can avoid the destructive nature of covetousness and foster a community based on love and respect.

As we conclude our exploration of the Ten Commandments, we see that each commandment is rooted in the theology of love. The tenth commandment teaches us about the importance of contentment and gratitude in our lives. May we respond to this call with hearts full of love and contentment, living out the principles of the tenth commandment in our daily lives and contributing to a culture of gratitude and respect?

EXPOSITORY STUDY AND COMPREHENSIVE COMMENTARY VERSE 17

Verse 17:

"Thou shalt not covet thy neighbor's house, thou shalt not covet thy neighbor's wife, nor his manservant, nor his maidservant, nor his ox, nor his ass, nor anything that is thy neighbor's."

King James Bible's Reference:

"Thou shalt not covet thy neighbor's house, thou shalt not covet thy neighbor's wife, nor his manservant, nor his maidservant, nor his ox, nor his ass, nor anything that is thy neighbor's." (Exodus 20:17, KJV)

Interpretation:

Exodus 20:17 contains the tenth commandment, which deals with the inner attitude of covetousness. This commandment forbids desiring or longing for anything that belongs to another person, emphasizing moral and ethical boundaries concerning possessions and relationships.

Commentary:

"Thou shalt not covet thy neighbor's house": The commandment begins by addressing the desire for one's neighbor's primary possession—their home. Coveting a neighbor's house represents a longing for the stability, status, or comfort that one perceives in the life of another (Luke 12:15).

"Thou shalt not covet thy neighbour's wife": This extends the prohibition to personal relationships, highlighting the sanctity of marriage and the importance of respecting others' intimate bonds (Matthew 5:28).

"Nor his manservant, nor his maidservant, nor his ox, nor his ass": The inclusion of servants and working animals underscores the comprehensive nature of the commandment, covering all forms of property that contribute to one's livelihood and well-being (Colossians 3:5).

"Nor anything that is thy neighbor's": The commandment concludes with a general prohibition against coveting anything that belongs to another person, emphasizing a principle of contentment and respect for others' rights (Hebrews 13:5).

Concordance:

- Thou shalt not covet: This phrase establishes the principle of guarding against the internal sin of desire for what others possess, promoting contentment and ethical behavior (Romans 7:7; Romans 13:9).

- Thy neighbor's house/wife/servants/animals: These specific prohibitions illustrate the wide range of areas where covetousness can manifest, from material possessions to intimate relationships (Deuteronomy 5:21).

References from the King James Bible:

1. Luke 12:15: "And he said unto them, Take heed, and beware of covetousness: for a man's life consisteth not in the abundance of the things which he possesseth."

2. Matthew 5:28: "But I say unto you, That whosoever looketh on a woman to lust after her hath committed adultery with her already in his heart."

3. Colossians 3:5: "Mortify therefore your members which are upon the earth; fornication, uncleanness, inordinate affection, evil concupiscence, and covetousness, which is idolatry."

4. Hebrews 13:5: "Let your conversation be without covetousness, and be content with such things as ye have: for he hath said, I will never leave thee, nor forsake thee."

5. Romans 7:7: "What shall we say then? Is the law a sin? God forbid. Nay, I had not known sin, but by the law: for I had not known lust, except the law had said, Thou shalt not covet."

6. Romans 13:9: "For this, Thou shalt not commit adultery, Thou shalt not kill, Thou shalt not steal, Thou shalt not bear false witness, Thou shalt not covet; and if there be any other commandments, it is briefly comprehended in this saying, namely, Thou shalt love thy neighbor as thyself."

Interpretation and Application:

- Internal Discipline: The tenth commandment emphasizes the importance of controlling internal desires and thoughts, recognizing that sin often begins in the heart.

- Respect for Others' Rights: By forbidding covetousness, the commandment promotes respect for the property and relationships of others, which is foundational for social harmony and justice.

- Contentment and Gratitude: This commandment encourages believers to cultivate contentment and gratitude for what they have, rather than longing for what others possess, aligning with a life of faith and trust in God's provisions.

Is there anything specific you would like to explore further in this verse or its implications for the spiritual and ethical life?

Let's delve deeper into the ethical and spiritual implications of Exodus 20:17, the commandment against coveting, and how it shapes our understanding of personal conduct and social ethics.

Spiritual Implications

1. Heart Condition: Exodus 20:17 challenges the condition of the heart, focusing on internal motivations rather than just external actions. It highlights the biblical truth that sin begins in the heart. This is reinforced in the New Testament, where Jesus often speaks to the importance of one's heart intentions (Matthew 5:28). The commandment invites a deep self-examination of one's desires and motivations, encouraging a transformation that aligns with godly values.

2. Relationship with God: Covetousness can be seen as a form of idolatry, where desire for other things or

relationships supersedes one's devotion to God. Colossians 3:5 explicitly labels covetousness as idolatry. The command helps believers to prioritize their relationship with God, recognizing Him as the ultimate source of fulfillment and satisfaction, rather than earthly possessions or relationships.

3. Spiritual Discipline: Adhering to this commandment requires the cultivation of spiritual disciplines like contentment, gratitude, and trust in God's provision. Philippians 4:11-13 discusses learning to be content in all circumstances, which is a direct antidote to covetousness. It's about finding peace and satisfaction in what we have been blessed with, rather than being consumed by desires for what others have.

Ethical Implications

1. Social Harmony: By instructing not to covet anything that belongs to another, this commandment lays a foundation for peace and harmony within the community. When individuals refrain from coveting, it reduces conflicts, jealousy, and strife, which often stem from desires for others' possessions or status. This principle supports the broader biblical call to love one's neighbor and seek their welfare.

2. Justice and Equity: Covetousness can lead to actions that disrupt social justice and equity—such as theft, fraud, and other forms of injustice. By curbing the desire to covet, the

commandment indirectly promotes justice and fairness in dealings with others. It upholds the dignity of others by respecting their rights to personal property and relationships.

3. Economic Ethics: From an economic standpoint, non-covetous behavior encourages fair business practices and discourages unethical methods of gaining wealth. It fosters an environment where people are valued over possessions, and where economic actions are guided by integrity rather than greed.

Practical Applications

1. Mindfulness and Meditation: Practicing mindfulness can help in becoming more aware of one's thoughts and desires. Meditating on scriptures that promote contentment and trust in God can reshape desires according to godly values.

2. Community Engagement: Engaging in community and church activities can shift focus from personal desires to the needs of others. Service to others is a powerful way to combat the self-centeredness that covetousness breeds.

3. Financial Stewardship: Adopting a lifestyle of simplicity and stewardship can be a practical response to the commandment against covetousness. This might involve regular giving, ethical investing, and avoiding consumer debt, which often stems from coveting.

Exodus 20:17, therefore, not only prohibits a specific negative behavior but also encourages a positive, flourishing life centered on godly values and community well-being. It calls for a heart aligned with God's desires, where personal satisfaction comes from one's relationship with God and service to others rather than accumulation of possessions or status.

CHAPTER 12

CONCLUSION: THE TEN COMMANDMENTS AS A UNIFIED THEOLOGY OF LOVE

The Ten Commandments stand as one of the most profound and enduring ethical codes in human history. Given to Moses on Mount Sinai, these commandments have shaped the moral and spiritual foundations of countless generations. When viewed through the lens of love, the Ten Commandments reveal a divine blueprint for a life rooted in love for God and for others. They guide us in building a society where love, respect, and reverence are foundational principles. By embracing the love inherent in these commandments, we draw closer to understanding the heart of God and living out His greatest commandments: to love Him and to love our neighbors as ourselves.

The Commandments and Love for God

The first four commandments focus on our relationship with God, emphasizing love, reverence, and devotion. They set the foundation for a life dedicated to worshiping and honoring God, and they reveal the importance of putting God at the center of our lives.

1. The First Commandment: Love and Allegiance to God

- "You shall have no other gods before me."

- This commandment calls for exclusive devotion to God, recognizing Him as the one true God deserving of our ultimate love and allegiance.

2. The Second Commandment: Love through Worship

- "You shall not make for yourself a carved image..."

- This commandment warns against idolatry, preserving the purity of our relationship with God by worshiping Him as He truly is.

3. The Third Commandment: Love and Reverence for God's Name

- "You shall not take the name of the Lord your God in vain..."

- Respecting God's name is an act of love, reflecting our deep reverence for His holiness and authority.

4. The Fourth Commandment: Love and Rest in God

- "Remember the Sabbath day, to keep it holy."

- The Sabbath is a gift of rest, reflecting God's love and care for us. By observing the Sabbath, we express our love for God and trust in His provision.

The Commandments and Love for Others

The remaining six commandments focus on our relationships with others, emphasizing respect, integrity, and compassion. They provide practical guidelines for living out love in our interactions with those around us.

5. The Fifth Commandment: Love and Honor for Parents

- "Honor your father and your mother..."

- This commandment underscores the importance of family and the respect and love owed to parents, promoting harmony and respect within the family unit.

6. The Sixth Commandment: Love and the Sanctity of Life

- "You shall not murder."

- The sanctity of human life is paramount. This commandment calls us to value and protect life, fostering a community where love and respect for life prevail.

7. The Seventh Commandment: Love and Marital Faithfulness

- "You shall not commit adultery."

- Marital fidelity is a profound expression of love and commitment. This commandment protects the sanctity of marriage, encouraging trust, loyalty, and love between spouses.

8. The Eighth Commandment: Love and Respect for Others' Property

- "You shall not steal."

- Respecting others' property is an act of love and consideration, acknowledging the rights and dignity of others and fostering a community based on trust and mutual respect.

9. The Ninth Commandment: Love and Truthfulness

- "You shall not bear false witness against your neighbor."

- Truthfulness is a cornerstone of loving relationships. This commandment promotes honesty and integrity, essential for trust and love within any community.

10. The Tenth Commandment: Love and Contentment

- "You shall not covet..."

- Contentment reflects a heart at peace, free from envy and greed. This commandment encourages us to appreciate what we have and to cultivate a loving and grateful heart, avoiding the destructive nature of covetousness.

The Unified Theology of Love

Together, the Ten Commandments present a unified theology of love. They teach us that true love for God and others is expressed through our actions, attitudes, and relationships. The commandments guide us in living a life that honors God and respects the dignity and worth of every person.

Jesus summarized the essence of the Ten Commandments with the greatest commandments: "Love the Lord your God with all your heart and with all your soul and with all your mind" and "Love your neighbor as yourself" (Matthew 22:37-39). These two commandments encapsulate the heart of the Decalogue, revealing that love is the fulfillment of the law.

Building a Society on Love and Respect

By embracing the love inherent in the Ten Commandments, we can build a society based on love and respect. These commandments provide a moral framework that promotes justice, peace, and well-being. They call us to:

1. Prioritize Relationships: Recognize the importance of our relationships with God and others. Prioritize love, respect, and compassion in all our interactions.

2. Promote Justice and Fairness: Uphold principles of justice and fairness in our communities. Advocate for the

rights and dignity of all individuals, ensuring that everyone is treated with respect and equity.

3. Foster Trust and Integrity: Cultivate trust and integrity in our personal and communal lives. Be honest, transparent, and accountable in all our dealings.

4. Embrace Contentment and Gratitude: Cultivate a heart of contentment and gratitude. Appreciate the blessings in our lives and avoid the pitfalls of envy and greed.

5. Seek Peace and Reconciliation: Strive for peace and reconciliation in our relationships. Address conflicts with empathy and understanding, seeking to restore harmony and build stronger bonds.

Drawing Closer to the Heart of God

Embracing the Ten Commandments as a theology of love draws us closer to the heart of God. These commandments reveal God's character and His desire for us to live in loving relationship with Him and with one another. By living out these principles, we reflect God's love and bring His light into the world.

As we conclude our exploration of the Ten Commandments, let us remember that they are not just rules to follow but expressions of divine love. May we strive to live out these commandments with hearts full of love and gratitude, building a society where love, respect, and reverence are foundational principles. In doing so, we fulfill God's greatest commandments and draw closer to understanding His heart and His purpose for our lives.